No Longer Outsiders

D1019451

No Longer Outsiders

Black and Latino Interest Group Advocacy on Capitol Hill

MICHAEL D. MINTA

The University of Chicago Press
Chicago and London

The University of Chicago Press, Chicago 60637
The University of Chicago Press, Ltd., London
© 2021 by The University of Chicago
All rights reserved. No part of this book may be used or reproduced in any manner whatsoever without written permission, except in the case of brief quotations in critical articles and reviews. For more information, contact the University of Chicago Press, 1427 E. 60th St., Chicago, IL 60637.
Published 2021
Printed in the United States of America

30 29 28 27 26 25 24 23 22 21   1 2 3 4 5

ISBN-13: 978-0-226-76527-3 (cloth)
ISBN-13: 978-0-226-76530-3 (paper)
ISBN-13: 978-0-226-76544-0 (e-book)
DOI: https://doi.org/10.7208/chicago/9780226765440.001.0001

Library of Congress Cataloging-in-Publication Data

Names: Minta, Michael D., 1969– author.
Title: No longer outsiders : Black and Latino interest group advocacy on
    Capitol Hill / Michael D. Minta.
Description: Chicago : University of Chicago Press, 2021. | Includes
    bibliographical references and index.
Identifiers: LCCN 2020043066 | ISBN 9780226765273 (cloth) |
    ISBN 9780226765303 (paperback) | ISBN 9780226765440 (e-book)
Subjects: LCSH: United States. Congress. | Public interest lobbying—United
    States. | Pressure groups—United States. | Human rights advocacy—United
    States. | African Americans—Civil rights—Societies, etc. | Latin Americans—
    Civil rights—United States—Societies, etc. | Minority legislators—United
    States. | Cultural pluralism—Political aspects—United States.
Classification: LCC JK1118.M56 2021 | DDC 328.73/07808996073—dc23
LC record available at https://lccn.loc.gov/2020043066

♾ This paper meets the requirements of ANSI/NISO Z39.48-1992 (Permanence of Paper).

CONTENTS

ONE

Introduction

In 2010, President Barack Obama signed the Fair Sentencing Act. The law reduced disparities in sentencing for convictions involving crack and powder cocaine. Prior to the passage of the act, anyone convicted of possessing, manufacturing, or trafficking five grams of crack received a mandatory five-year minimum prison sentence, the same as a person convicted of possessing, manufacturing, and trafficking five hundred grams of powder cocaine. The Fair Sentencing Act eliminated the mandatory-minimum sentences for simple possession and granted judges more discretion to determine appropriate sentencing. The law reduced the ratio of quantity of crack to quantity of powder cocaine from one hundred to one to eighteen to one by increasing the amount of crack needed to trigger a mandatory five-year sentence for trafficking or manufacturing from five grams to twenty-eight grams. The amount needed to trigger a similar sentence for powder cocaine remained the same, at five hundred grams.

The passage of the Fair Sentencing Act marked an important victory for civil rights organizations, which had argued that the mandatory federal drug sentences were unfair to racial and ethnic minorities. Since 1993, the National Association for the Advancement of Colored People (NAACP), the Leadership Conference for Civil Rights (LCCR), and the U.S. Sentencing Commission had been part of a coalition instrumental in keeping this issue before Congress. In the 1995, the NAACP's main lobbyist, Wade Henderson, testified in Congress before the House Judiciary Committee in support of eliminating the sentencing disparities, citing a U.S. Sentencing Commission report that showed their disproportionate impact on African Americans. According to Henderson, even though blacks accounted for only 26 percent of crack users, they represented 83 percent of individuals incarcerated in federal prison for possession of crack. From 1990 to 2015, the elimination of drug-related sentencing disparities was a top legislative priority of the NAACP. Through testimony at hearings and the publication of issue papers, the NAACP pushed for legislation, gathering legislative allies along the way. Henderson would later continue his advocacy efforts for sentencing reform as director of the LCCR. The NAACP and LCCR built a coalition of bipartisan support in Congress, where their greatest ally was the Congressional Black Caucus (CBC).

Congressman Charles Rangel (D-NY), one of the founders of the CBC in 1971, became a fierce champion of eliminating sentencing disparities. In the mid-1980s, Rangel, like many legislators, had favored a "get tough" attitude toward the drug problem, primarily due to the violence and devastation associated with the sale and use of crack in minority communities nationwide (Fortner 2015; Murakawa 2014). In 1990, the homicide rate for blacks in New York City was 35 deaths per 100,000—higher than it had been at any other time in history. Many experts attributed this high rate of violence to the sale and use of crack (Chauhan et al. 2011). Rangel initially supported the drug sentencing guidelines because he believed that federally imposed sentences would be fairer than sentences imposed by judges who had broad discretion. He later changed his position when research and advocacy groups found that blacks were charged and sentenced to prison time with disproportionate frequency under the new guidelines. As early as 1993, Rangel introduced a bill in Congress calling for the elimination of drug sentencing disparities between crack and powder cocaine, and he reintroduced the bill in each session of Congress from 1993 to 2010. Democratic senators including Russ Feingold (D-WI) and Dick Durbin (D-IL) sponsored companion bills in the U.S. Senate. The advocacy of civil rights organizations and these coalition partners in Congress ultimately led to the passage of the Fair Sentencing Act.

It is not unusual for organizations to build successful coalitions both inside and outside of Congress in order to advance their policy preferences. What was different in the passage of the Fair Sentencing Act, however, was the activist role that the CBC played in the process. CBC members did not receive large campaign contributions from minority civil rights organizations, nor did those organizations engage in significant social protests to bring national attention to the sentencing issue in order to force Congress to act. Despite not being subjected to these methods that groups commonly use to apply pressure, CBC members were just as active in keeping sentencing on the agenda as civil rights organizations were. Not only did Rep. Rangel (D-NY) sponsor the bill and introduce it repeatedly over seventeen years, but other CBC members also introduced similar bills, including Rep. Maxine Waters (D-CA), Rep. Sheila Jackson Lee (D-TX), and Rep. Robert Scott (D-VA). The CBC became a forceful advocate for sentencing reform. While many white Democrats cosponsored legislation, very few sponsored similar legislation on their own. Minority civil rights organizations' advocacy efforts for sentencing reform were subsidized almost entirely by CBC members.

Although groups like the NAACP and the LCCR are known best for their participation in the social movement protests and legal battles of the 1950s and 1960s and have been successful in using protests to influence congressional behavior (see, e.g., Gillion 2013; McAdam 1982; Morris 1984), it is less well known that these groups expend considerable effort lobbying legislators on Capitol Hill (Francis 2014; Sullivan 2009; Watson 1990; Zelizer 2004). The passage of the Civil Rights Act of 1964 and the Voting Rights Act (VRA) of 1965—and subsequent language-provision amendments to the VRA—incorporated blacks and Latinos into the formal political system. As a result, the national bargaining power and leverage of groups such as the NAACP, UnidosUS (formerly the National Council of La Raza), and the Mexican American Legal Defense and Educational Fund (MALDEF) improved. No longer could legislators afford to ignore the policy issues of black and Latino voters without repercussions at the ballot box.

The work of the NAACP and LCCR in favor of passage of the Fair Sentencing Act was typical of these groups' activities, which occur largely outside of public view. For this reason, the scope and influence of their efforts, as well as the efforts of their legislative advocates, are not readily understood or even known. Because their activities are discreet, civil rights groups are frequently criticized by the general public for their alleged inaction or ineffectiveness in representing minority interests. Nor are citizens the only ones with pessimistic views of civil rights advocacy. Political scientists and legal scholars have argued that civil rights organizations do not devote sufficient attention and resources to controversial problems such as criminal justice or public health issues (Alexander 2010; Cohen 1999; Strolovitch 2007). In addition, some political scientists and sociologists have found that civil rights groups are largely concerned with organizational maintenance and have become less concerned over time with advancing progressive policy (Marquez 2003; Piven and Cloward 1977).

Not only are civil rights groups viewed as generally ineffective in representing black and Latino interests; legal scholars have also argued that the legal strategy pursued by civil rights organizations to increase the number of blacks elected to Congress has done little to advance the substantive policy interests of underrepresented minorities (Guinier 1994). Indeed, in

Tyranny of the Majority, Lani Guinier (1994) argued that black electoral success has not ensured broad participation by blacks in politics or advanced progressive policy change.

Many of the legal scholars and political scientists mentioned here examine similar and sometimes overlapping issues regarding group effectiveness and minority representation, but rarely do they talk to one another. The result is that we are left with an incomplete accounting of whether civil rights groups represent the interests of blacks and Latinos and are influential in drawing attention to their issues in Congress. Moreover, we do not know whether their strategy to increase the number of blacks and Latinos in Congress has paid off in terms of these groups achieving greater legislative success in Congress. Scholars have not comprehensively assessed the legislative effectiveness of civil rights organizations, in part because many of the measures that scholars use to assess group influence do not apply to nonprofit groups with 501(c)(3) public charity status—which includes civil rights organizations. Academic studies that focus on contributions to political candidates and public declarations of lobbying activity, which find that money is vital to getting members of Congress to pursue interest group policy preferences, are limited in their ability to provide insight into those nonprofit groups banned by federal law from contributing directly to political candidates or carrying out extensive lobbying—although it is important to note that these groups do conduct a wide range of policy advocacy activities that serve the same function as lobbying.

The main enterprise of this book is to provide a comprehensive account of the effectiveness of the advocacy efforts of minority civil rights organizations and their legislative allies. Specifically, I examine how black and Latino civil rights organizations exert influence in the legislative process despite the limits placed on their lobbying and their inability to contribute to political candidates. I do this through a systematic study of the role, if any, that the racial and ethnic diversity of House membership plays in helping civil rights groups get Congress to address their issues. Are civil rights groups successful in advancing the policy they champion in the legislative process? Specifically, do the issues that civil rights groups care about receive greater attention in a more racially and ethnically diverse House than in a chamber that is less diverse? I find that diversity in Congress is responsible for greater influence and policy success for minority civil rights organizations, particularly in the U.S. House of Representatives.

This finding is particularly notable because diversity has been achieved in Congress not only through demographic changes in Northern cities and the liberalization of citizens' attitudes toward minority rights but also through the work of civil rights groups themselves. Black, Latino, and liberal white civil rights organizations have been pivotal in creating the very diversity that enhances their access to and policy success in Congress. In the 1980s and 1990s, these groups initiated lawsuits that created the majority-black and majority-Latino districts that have increased the racial and ethnic diversity of state legislatures and the U.S. House of Representatives (Davidson and Grofman 1994; Guinier 1994; Kousser 1999).

Although the VRA granted entry into formal politics for civil rights groups and raised the expectation of blacks and other minorities that civil rights groups would be more successful in Congress, there is as yet no systematic evidence that civil rights groups are more successful today than they were before the passage of civil rights laws. This study provides clear evidence of the efficacy of civil rights organizations' congressional influence by measuring the relationship between minority representation in Congress and the frequency of legislators' advocacy for civil rights groups' policy priorities.

Background

The passage of the Civil Rights Act of 1964 and the Voting Rights Act of 1965 marked the legislative high point of the civil rights movement for underrepresented groups in the United States. Although the civil rights movement focused mostly on the rights of African Americans, many other underrepresented groups, including Latinos, Asian Americans, and women, also became protected classes under the landmark legislation. Prominent civil rights organizations such as the NAACP, National Urban League (NUL), Southern Christian Leadership Conference (SCLC), Congress of Racial Equality (CORE), and Student Non-Violent Coordinating Committee (SNCC) placed significant pressure on Congress and the president to pass this important legislation.

Although the civil rights movement of the 1950s and 1960s, commonly called the "Second Reconstruction," receives much of scholarly attention, civil rights advocacy for blacks and Latinos has been a long and arduous struggle. For blacks, the Reconstruction Era of the mid- to late 1800s, immediately following Emancipation and the end of the Civil War, marked the entry of the freedman into U.S. civil society. Led by Sen. Charles Sumner (D-MA) and Rep. Thaddeus Stevens (D-PA)—the so-called Radical Republicans in Congress—the federal government passed the Thirteenth, Fourteenth, and Fifteenth Amendments to the U.S. Constitution, also known as the War Amendments, which abolished the institution of slavery, established citizenship for blacks, and granted suffrage to black men. Black men were subsequently elected to Congress, and the institution passed several bills aimed at solidifying the civil rights of blacks, as well as providing economic relief and assistance to the freedmen (Foner 1988). These gains were short lived, however, as eventually the GOP abandoned its commitment to securing civil rights and political rights for blacks (James and Lawson 1999; Valelly 2004). The rise of the Jim Crow South from the 1870s through the 1960s and the power of Southern Democrats in Congress made it difficult for minorities to obtain civil rights through the mechanisms of state or federal government.

The advocacy efforts of the NAACP, founded in New York in 1909 by white and black activists in response to racial violence, were met with fierce resistance in the legislative arena. The NAACP had little success getting Congress to advance its policy priorities, such as passing legislation to eliminate discrimination in housing and employment. Despite these obstacles, and although it had limited power to influence legislators' electoral prospects because of black voters' effective disenfranchisement in the Jim Crow era, the NAACP continued to lobby members of Congress. The NAACP was outlawed in the South, and black Southerners had to rely on its political strength in Northern areas, where blacks were gaining power (McAdam 1982; Morris 1984). Civil rights groups used the courts and outsider lobbying tactics such as protests to attract national attention. The NAACP led a strong lobbying effort to pass antilynching legislation in the 1910s to 1940s. As a result of its efforts and the antilynching movement, the House forwarded antilynching legislation in 1922, although the Senate did not pass the bill (Francis 2014).

By the 1930s, the NAACP had decided to focus on litigation as its primary tool for gaining civil rights protections for blacks (Bateman, Katznelson, and Lapinski 2018; Francis 2014; Sullivan 2009). The group's leaders did not abandon lobbying tactics in Congress, but they directed more resources to the legal side, as the courts were a more sympathetic audience. The NAACP and other civil rights groups fought to eliminate the filibuster in the Senate and to find mechanisms to hold legislators accountable for their voting decisions (Zelizer 2004). The LCCR established roll-call voting report cards to publicize legislators' positions on legislation. The NAACP's prior efforts on civil rights set the stage for the passage of the Civil Rights Act (1964) and Voting Rights Act (1965).

Alongside the NAACP, several other mainstream civil rights organizations got their start in the early 1900s, including the League of United Latin American Citizens (LULAC) and the American GI Forum, both of which fought for civil rights for Mexican Americans. From the 1920s through the 1960s, while the NAACP took on discrimination, racist violence, and voter suppression on behalf of black Americans, LULAC and the GI Forum argued that Latinos should not be segregated or treated differently from Anglos, because Mexican Americans were white also. The leaders of LULAC and the GI Forum did not see Latinos as a separate racial minority group, nor did those leaders want to be identified as people of Mexican heritage (Behnken 2011; Kaplowitz 2005). LULAC strongly opposed guest-worker programs and supported Operation Wetback, which sent many Mexican workers and some Mexican citizens back to Mexico. LULAC and the GI Forum leaders rejected any association with the black civil rights struggle and focused on using an assimilationist, or "whiteness," strategy (Behnken 2011; Kaplowitz 2005). During this time, most of the advocacy of LULAC and the GI Forum took place at the local level, only rarely involving protests. LULAC's efforts to desegregate schools, for example, occurred mostly locally through negotiation directly with officials, although its efforts sometimes also involved legal action. And although LULAC did not spend much time lobbying the federal government, the GI Forum did lobby to ensure that Mexican American veterans received the same benefits as white veterans.

During the 1960s, however, several Latino national organizations rejected the assimilationist philosophy of LULAC and began demanding that the federal government get involved to protect Mexican Americans as an ethnic group separate from whites and blacks. Latino civil rights organizations such as UnidosUS and the Mexican American Legal Defense and Educational Fund were organized in 1968. These organizations made demands for Latinos to be included as a language minority deserving of civil rights protections.

The advocacy efforts of civil rights groups like the NAACP and LULAC have always been a subject of regulatory concern. In the 1940s and 1950s, the NAACP's Washington Bureau requested information from the NAACP's Legal Defense Fund on whether the bureau should report its advocacy work through lobbying disclosure forms. Much discussion ensued between Thurgood Marshall, then chief counsel of the NAACP, and executive director Leslie Perry regarding whether the NAACP was required to register as a lobbying organization and whether advocacy was the same as lobbying.[1] This concern of the NAACP was not unwarranted: the U.S. attorney general had sent a letter to the NAACP requesting more information about the group's lobbying activity. In the 1980s, the NAACP was questioned several times about its advocacy activities and received threats that it might lose its 501(c)(3) status. In 1979, the NAACP passed a resolution stating that reporting on its visits to federal officials would hinder its advocacy efforts.

Advocacy by 501(c)(3) and 501(c)(4) organizations is a difficult balancing act. Most of these groups do not want to jeopardize their tax-exempt status, and thus they may understate the amount of lobbying that occurs on the Hill, or they may fail to get involved in lobbying at all. In an interview I conducted with one staffer at a civil rights organization, the staffer told me that only one person was devoted specifically to lobbying—although the staffer did not use the specific term "lobbying"—on behalf of the organization. Staff from the organization could meet with federal officials to provide information about an issue that concerned the group, but they could not urge members to either support or oppose a bill. In this way, civil rights groups' "advocacy" work is the means by which they contact, inform, and subsidize the work of legislative allies. Large organizations such as the NAACP and UnidosUS must pursue advocacy without crossing the lobbying thresholds established in the U.S. Tax Code and enforced by the Internal Revenue Service (IRS). The thresholds for nonprofit lobbying can further limit their actions.

The Lobbying Disclosure Act of 1995 (LDA) provides a narrow definition of lobbying. Groups have to spend $20,000 within a six-month period even to be required to report on their lobbying activity; many groups fail to meet this threshold and thereby escape federal monitoring. In addition, activities such as testifying at hearings are not considered lobbying, but rather providing information. Because the IRS rules are narrow in scope, lobbying disclosure reports (LDRs) may fail to capture the true amount of lobbying groups engage in. Berry and Arons (2003) note that a group can draft a bill for a member of Congress, and this is not considered lobbying if the member requested the action. When legislators request briefings, summaries, or other important information about a bill, this is not considered lobbying either. If a group initiates contact with the official, however, then the contact is considered lobbying under federal law and IRS rules, and if the group's total lobbying activity meets the threshold, it must submit an LDR. The IRS rules allow for such distinctions—which become distinctions without meaning, even as civil rights organizations must adjust their tactics to accommodate them.

Challenges of Assessing Interest Group Success and Influence

For interest groups to achieve legislative success, they must first gain access to legislators. They employ a variety of methods to do so. First, they establish a reputation that makes legislators believe that working and cooperating with them will produce an electoral advantage (Hansen 1991). That is, groups must demonstrate that the information they provide to legislators is credible and will help get the legislators reelected. If the information is not reliable and does not help, then legislators will deny access.

Second, and most often cited, money gives interest groups access to members of Congress. This money can come through campaign contributions to political candidates or be spent on lobbying activity. Groups that contribute money to legislators' reelection campaigns or political action committees (PACs) are more likely to gain access to members than are groups that do not contribute; once groups have access, they attempt to exert influence on the legislative process, whether by getting legislators to vote in their preferred direction or by encouraging them to participate more on the issues of interest to the group that come before committees (Hall and Wayman 1990).

If contributing to candidates' campaigns were a prerequisite for organizations to gain access to legislators and thereby increase their odds of legislative success, then civil rights groups would be greatly hampered. They are outnumbered and outmatched in resources by groups that generally oppose their interests in the legislative arena (Schlozman 1984; Schlozman and Tierney 1986; Strolovitch 2007; Walker 1983). Business organizations, including oil and gas or Wall Street firms, spend billions of dollars donating to political action committees to influence public policy. In 2018, the U.S. Chamber of Commerce (USCC) contributed almost $400,000 to political candidates, compared to zero dollars contributed by civil rights groups.[2] Most of the money donated by the USCC went to candidates who opposed issues favored by minority civil rights groups.

Although civil rights groups are outspent in lobbying and are barred from contributing to political action committees, the extant research has not demonstrated whether this resource disparity hinders their ability to be successful. One of the greatest challenges in determining whether groups are effective in influencing congressional behavior is defining influence and finding reliable measures to capture it. Decades of studies have focused on whether donations from PACs to electoral campaigns are significant in biasing legislators' voting behavior, for example. Although some of these studies have found evidence that PAC contributions from organized interest groups in a variety of industries were successful in getting legislators to vote in the groups' preferred direction or even participate more in committee hearings (Hall and Wayman 1990), equally persuasive studies show that PAC contributions have minimal influence (Grenzke 1989; Hojnacki and Kimball 2001). The major problem with most of these studies is the difficulty in determining causality. That is, it is unclear whether legislators vote in the preferred direction of an organized interest because they have received contributions from it, or whether organized interests give money to legislators who are already predisposed to vote in favor of that interest. Even though Austen-Smith and Wright (1994) found that some organized groups gave money to undecided legislators and opposing legislators, we know that organized interest groups usually donate to their political allies and rarely give to or lobby undecided legislators or political opponents (Bauer, Pool, and Dexter 1963; Hall and Deardorff 2006; Hojnacki and Kimball 2001; Hojnacki and Kimball 1998). This is a significant challenge for scholarship that attempts to unpack the power of organized groups in federal policy making.

As I have touched on, a second challenge faces scholars who seek to study the influence of civil rights groups or citizen groups: PAC contributions cannot be used to assess influence by citizen groups on legislative behavior because the federal government legally bars citizen groups with public charity purposes—that is, with 501(c)(3) status—from contributing to political candidates and political action committees (Berry and Arons 2003). Possessing public charity status creates an opportunity in that it allows groups to receive charitable contributions and thus increase the size of their overall budget, but it also limits their ability to influence politics by donating to candidates.

The inability of civil rights organizations to contribute to political candidates might not be as problematic as it seems, however; friendly legislators are not likely to be swayed by vast sums of money coming from wealthy groups that oppose their interests. In fact, it is unlikely that the political opponents of civil rights organizations will even contribute to the organizations' political allies. Moreover, even if civil rights groups were able to donate to political candidates, it is unclear that they would be more successful. Organizations usually donate to their allies, which makes it very difficult to determine whether the money they donate is indeed influencing how legislators vote. Although analysis of PAC contributions cannot be used to attempt to determine the influence of civil rights groups, perhaps such an analysis would not meaningfully be able to tease apart a causal relationship in any event.

A third way in which interest groups can gain access to legislators is through lobbying members of Congress. The amount of lobbying a group can do is determined by its type of organization, its financial resources, and its organizational strength. On this metric, civil rights groups tend to have fewer resources, including smaller lobbying staffs and budgets, than do their business counterparts (Baumgartner and Leech 1998; Berry 1999; Schlozman 1984; Strolovitch 2007). In 2010, for example, the U.S. Chamber of Commerce spent more than $132 million in lobbying Congress, while the NAACP, UnidosUS, and LCCR combined spent only $2.1 million.[3] And again, just as the nonprofit designation bars groups from giving to candidates, the law restricts how much effort civil rights organizations, as nonprofit groups, can devote toward lobbying federal officials (Berry and Arons 2003). Groups can devote only a small percentage of their activities to lobbying. As a result, civil rights groups de-emphasize how much time they actually spend on lobbying legislators for fear that the IRS will revoke their tax-exempt status. Instead, minority-focused 501(c)(3)s encourage legislators to claim credit for activism on the issues these organizations support, thus minimizing the groups' participation in activities that would need to be reported under the lobbying disclosure laws. Hilary Shelton, the head lobbyist for the NAACP's Washington Bureau, sums up the philosophy of many lobbyists for not-for-profit groups, and why it is difficult to gauge the lobbying influence of civil rights organizations: "There's nothing you can't get done if you're willing to let someone else get credit for it."[4]

Thus, in the case of civil rights organizations, it becomes necessary to reassess the concept of influence itself, as well as how it might be measured. Such an investigation is timely: although empirical findings support the contention that groups with more resources exert more power, a growing body of research has challenged this supposition. Scholars have found, for example, that resource-rich groups can rarely use lobbying to get their preferred policy outcome because mass opinion limits the influence of powerful business groups in congressional policy making (Smith 2000). Resource-rich groups are usually not cohesive on many policy issues, and some align in their policy interests with resource-poor groups (Baumgartner et al. 2009). These studies begin to point to an equal playing field, or at least a playing field that is more equal than the resource differential would suggest. It is worth asking this: if civil rights groups are successful even with fewer resources than their opponents, then how do they achieve this success? Developing robust measures of civil rights organizations' influence and analyzing whether and to what extent they succeed in pushing their policy priorities promises to provide a wealth of information about the exercise of congressional influence from an angle that has previously received little attention.

Of course, civil rights groups might successfully push their policy priorities without adequately forwarding the priorities of the voters they purport to represent. The political representation literature focuses extensively on whether the race or ethnicity of legislators matters in the representation of minority interests in Congress, but research on whether civil rights organizations are effective in representing and advancing minority interests at the federal level is in the early stages. Those scholars who have studied the question focus on issues that tend to divide minority constituencies, such as gay and lesbian rights and some social welfare policies (Cohen 1999; Martinez 2009; Marquez 1993; Kaplowitz 2005; Pinderhughes 1995; Strolovitch 2007), but they do not address how successful civil rights groups are in advancing policies in the legislative arena that have widespread minority support. The extant literature argues that advocacy efforts by the NAACP and LULAC do not adequately represent the interests of all blacks and Latinos, reaffirming Schattschneider (1960) and others who state that the advocacy efforts of organized groups are biased toward the interests of upper-class or more advantaged members of these groups. Specifically, Cohen (1999) found that the NAACP and SCLC did not proactively advocate for members most at risk of contracting HIV/AIDS, despite their claims to represent all groups. Strolovitch (2007) similarly confirmed that many other minority groups represented the interests of the most advantaged while ignoring the interests of their disadvantaged members.

The extent to which Latino advocacy groups have been effective in advocating for Hispanic interests has also been challenged (Marquez 1993). According to Marquez, LULAC has not been effective since the 1970s because it stopped providing incentives to its members. Other scholars have challenged this assertion. Marquez is critical of Latino advocacy groups, claiming that their agenda is heavily influenced by foundations and corporations, and that this influence prevents them from spearheading progressive policy change that would have positive effects in the Latino community.

With the exception of Hero and Preuhs (2013), most political representation studies do not address the extent to which black and Latino organizations work together to advance common issues that apply to both groups. Hero and Preuhs comprehensively examine advocacy efforts by black and Latino groups, focusing on whether these groups form coalitions to work with each other at the federal level or whether they compete with one another. They found that these groups usually work in their own policy space. Sometimes they work together on issues of mutual concern, but normally they work separately, without conflict. This book builds on the work of Hero and Preuhs by examining how the presence of diverse congressional representatives affects policies supported by black and Latino advocacy organizations.

Several key questions emerge from this review of the scholarship of interest group influence and civil rights organizations, first among them how effective and successful minority civil rights organizations are at getting their stated legislative priorities enacted into policy. Are civil rights groups more successful now that blacks are formally incorporated into the political system than they were when blacks were excluded? If so, how are civil rights groups successful despite their financial limitations? How and when are they most effective? In addition, it is worth investigating whether minority civil rights groups are effective at representing all members of their stated constituencies. Do they represent the interests of a broader minority constituency, or do they focus on a narrow, privileged subset?

Theory

Civil rights organizations demonstrate influence in Congress that cannot be captured easily through traditional measures. I argue that the success of these groups should be determined by examining whether greater racial and ethnic diversity in Congress has led to greater influence or policy success for advocacy groups in federal policy making. This argument grows out of my focus on the legal strategy used by civil rights organizations to increase the number of congressional advocates in order to improve congressional attention to their issues. Specifically, civil rights organizations have benefited from legal suits brought under the Voting Rights Act that increased the number of *legislative advocates*, or African American, Latino, and Asian American legislators in Congress. In addition to influencing political entities to create majority-minority districts, civil rights groups have also played a crucial role in the recruitment of candidates, with many minority candidates belonging to, or having once belonged to, these organizations (Minta 2011). The inclusion of more advocates in Congress, and the presence of strong ties to these advocates, enhances the lobbying effectiveness of civil rights organizations by creating a cadre of legislators who are willing to actively champion the policies and legislation of these groups and of minority constituents. Additionally, increasing the number of their advocates in Congress improves the odds of civil rights groups' legislative success by granting them more access to the legislative process. Advocates might press for key policies favored by civil rights organizations, such as legislation that reduces sentencing disparities between crack and powder cocaine or that enacts harsher penalties for hate crimes.

Another way of making this point is to argue that the influence of civil rights groups comes at the selection stage of the legislative process. The impact of lobbying at the later stages, such as a legislator's decision to vote in accordance with a civil rights organization's policy preferences, hold hearings or markups, or be active in committee on behalf on the organization, are indirect measures. In fact, Kingdon (1989) has argued that the most influence that constituents have on legislators is during the selection stage. Organizations also have the most impact at the early stage of a legislator's career rather than later (Fenno 1978; Fiorina 1974). Given that this is the case, the election of black and Latino legislators from newly formed majority-minority districts, along with the presence of existing minority legislators, should lead to the greater influence and success of civil rights organizations in Congress. These efforts highlight what Baumgartner and Jones (2002) refer to as positive feedback processes in politics, where action in one area, such as increasing the number of minority legislators in the House, should lead to greater policy success at other stages of federal policy making.

But by what mechanism does the election of more minority legislators lead to greater policy success for minority advocacy groups in Congress? Primarily, minority legislators become not simply allies but forceful advocates themselves on issues that mirror the policy preferences of civil rights organizations. Minority legislators allied with civil rights groups have organized into caucuses and established a strong organizational infrastructure that rivals the lobbying effectiveness of the traditional civil rights organizations. During the early years of the CBC, in fact, some of its members argued that they were better representatives of black interests than traditional civil rights groups such as the NAACP and NUL because they were directly elected by the people. Minority legislators are not passive observers in the civil rights struggle but primary players in the lobbying game. Unlike civil rights organizations, these groups are not subject to restrictions on how much they can lobby and advocate for issues that are important to minorities. Taking the Fair Sentencing Act as an example, CBC members such as Charles Rangel, Maxine Waters, and Bobby Scott were more inclined than white Democrats to support and fight for fair sentencing legislation.

Improvements to civil rights groups' access to members of Congress derives not only from increasing numbers of minority legislators but also from the development of informal networks between legislative advocates and the leaders of civil rights organizations. These networks arise, again, because many legislative advocates are, or once were, members of the civil rights organizations. Members of civil rights organizations ran for office in many of the newly created House districts, further strengthening the link between civil rights organizations and members of Congress. Black legislators such as James Clyburn (D-SC) and John Conyers (D-MI) were members of the NAACP; Eleanor Holmes Norton (D-DC) was the president of a college chapter of the NAACP and served as a staff attorney for the American Civil Liberties Union (ACLU) in the 1960s and 1970s. These legislative advocates, moreover, have established diversity infrastructures that assist in their advocacy for issues that directly relate to the agendas of civil rights organizations (Minta and Sinclair-Chapman 2013). Organizations such as the Congressional Black Caucus, the Congressional Hispanic Caucus, and the Congressional Asian and Pacific Islander Caucus were formed by minority legislators not just to represent the interests of blacks, Latinos, and Asian Americans in their own districts but also to represent the interests of all blacks, Latinos, and Asian Americans nationally (Clay 1993; Minta 2011; Tyson 2016). In 2005, minority legislators formed a separate caucus, the Congressional Tri-Caucus, in response to governmental failures following Hurricane Katrina and to facilitate agenda coordination across minority groups. Caucuses allow for the sharing of resources across legislative offices, and they enhance communication and information sharing and provide for the coordination of agendas and messages. Members use the information gained from caucus membership to assist in advocating for minority interests in House committees that have jurisdiction over civil rights, social welfare, health, and education. Consequently, civil rights groups do not need to spend as much money on lobbying as business interests do in order to exert influence.

In addition to benefiting from membership in informal networks, legislative advocates for civil rights groups from newly created House districts represent majority-black and majority-Latino constituencies, with more liberal policy preferences that are in line with the priorities of civil rights organizations. There is an electoral incentive for these legislators to pursue policies supported by civil rights organizations. Minta and Sinclair-Chapman (2013) found that the increase in racial and ethnic diversity in the U.S. House of Representatives was the primary reason the chamber began to pay greater attention to minority interests. It was civil rights organizations that were largely responsible for increasing diversity in the chamber (Davidson and Grofman 1994; Kousser 1999). Thus, we should expect civil rights groups to have greater access because of this network.[5]

This book contributes to the literature on minority representation by focusing on how increasing the number of minority legislators in Congress enhances the success of minority civil rights groups, which in turn improves the representation of minority interests in both chambers of Congress—the House and the Senate. This expectation is not unreasonable, considering that most of the research on the political representation of minorities demonstrates that having more minorities in Congress leads to better substantive representation of minority interests (Canon 1999; Casellas 2010; Dovi 2002; Hardy-Fanta, Lien, Pinderhughes, and Sierra 2016; Grose 2011; King-Meadows 2011; Mansbridge 1999; Minta and Brown 2014; Rouse 2013; Rivers 2012; Tate 2003; Tillery 2011; Wallace 2014). Although having more advocates in Congress does not guarantee the legislative success of civil rights groups, the expectation is that these groups' chances of success significantly improve. If an increase in minority advocates in Congress does not lead to positive outcomes for minority groups, then it should at least result in better representation of minority interests in the legislative arena. Although they are not perfectly aligned, the policy priorities of black and Latino legislators and civil rights organizations are very similar. Tate (2014) found that the CBC was less radical in the 2010s than in the 1970s, for example, but even so, the policy interests of the CBC and NAACP are closely aligned. This might speak to the NAACP itself modifying its strategy and becoming less radical than it was in the 1950s and 1960s.

This book demonstrates that the presence of more minority advocates in Congress increases the receptivity of the legislature to minority group interests. In terms of getting Congress to take action on a given bill, diversity is important, and not just in making minority sponsorship likely. The presence of minority interests advocating for minority-friendly policy can spur other legislators to act, particularly white legislators. Civil rights groups engage in the same activities as other citizen groups and business and professional organizations: they meet with legislators, write bills and amendments, and provide information to be used at legislative hearings. The key factor in their success, however, is that minority civil rights groups have more legislators who are willing to grant them access and to act on their legislative agenda, especially on racial issues. The CBC's involvement in the Fair Sentencing Act, for example, was critical to its passage. The Congressional Hispanic Caucus (CHC) has played a similar role and has been a leading ally to UnidosUS, LULAC, and MALDEF in advocating on the Hill for immigration reform and bilingual education.

A few challenges immediately arise to the theory laid out here, the first of which involves diversity and representation. Although I argue that a more diverse Congress leads to more influence and success for civil rights groups, some scholars have claimed that increased diversity might in fact diminish the substantive representation of minority-group interests (Cameron, Epstein, and O'Halloran 1996; Guinier 1994; Lublin 1997; Kanthak and Krause 2012; Overby and Cosgrove 1996; Shotts 2003; Swain 1993).

As the number of minorities in the legislature increases, majority-group male legislators become less likely to support women's interests, for example (Kanthak and Krause 2012). Some have argued that minority legislators will never move beyond token representation and thus will have difficulty getting majority-white group members to support the legislative agenda of blacks (Guinier 1994). Swain (1993) found that Democrats are primarily supportive of minority interests in Congress, and attempts to construct more majority-black and majority-Latino districts have diminished white Democrats' chances of winning office while increasing the odds that the GOP will take over the House. Thus, the strategy of civil rights organizations to increase the number of black and Latino legislators might be found to hurt Democrats and diminish support for civil rights groups' policy initiatives. I address this objection in the chapters to come, where I show that greater racial and ethnic committee diversity leads to more attention to bills favored by minority civil rights organizations, as well as more opportunities for these organizations to testify before Congress.

Additionally, although there is good reason to believe that civil rights organizations have a great deal of influence in Congress, especially in the civil rights policy area, empirically it is difficult to assign causality to this influence because groups usually lobby their friends. Again, given that civil rights organizations played a crucial role in creating the districts that elected their allies to Congress, measuring influence becomes even more difficult. With the Fair Sentencing Act, for example, we cannot definitively conclude that minority legislators participated in promoting the bill because of the influence of the NAACP. What is certain is that the redistricting efforts of civil rights organizations are responsible for infusing Congress with legislators who tend to support their initiatives—but we cannot disentangle the extent to which legislators would or would not have supported these issues on their own. The attempt to get to the bottom of this question obscures the main point, however: that minority civil rights groups are effective in getting their policy preferences addressed by the federal government. The source of a given idea and who can claim credit for its successful promotion is not as important as the fact of the legislation getting passed. As the NAACP lobbyist Hilary Shelton stated in a quotation cited earlier, groups can get much done if they are willing to let legislators claim the credit.

So how do we measure legislative success for interest groups? The passage into law of the Fair Sentencing Act of 2010 is a clear and simple example of legislative success. Even though the law did not completely eliminate the disparity between sentencing for crack and powder cocaine, civil rights groups and their legislative advocates could credibly claim that they reduced federal sentencing disparities. As a measure of interest group success, however, the passage of a law is a high bar to clear. If we accept this as our measure, we will find that most interest group actions are not successful—at least not over a given congressional term. It takes a long time for advocacy to lead to bills that become laws; most never do. In the 111th Congress (2009–2010), under unified Democratic Party control, members in the House and Senate introduced 10,616 public bills; of this total, 4,626, or 43.5 percent, received committee consideration, but only 366, or 3.4 percent, became law.[6] Democrats tend to be more aligned than Republicans on issues favored by civil rights organizations, but the committee consideration or bill passage rate is not considerably different when control of the government is divided between the two political parties. In the 112th Congress (2011–2012), 10,432 bills were introduced, and of this total, 6,062, or 58 percent, received committee consideration, but only 272, or 2.6 percent, became law. Thus, organizations must be realistic about what they can achieve and what qualifies as success.

Capturing legislative success is a multitiered process. The sentencing-disparities bill was introduced in 1993, but it did not become a law until 2010. Thus, other measures of success are necessary to assess the effectiveness of interest groups' advocacy efforts. The extent to which Congress pays attention to an issue and advances it through the legislative process is crucial in advocacy. Once the bill is referred to a committee, the likelihood of getting the committee to conduct a hearing or markup is important. This is a difficult hurdle: most bills die in committee. In this study, I define "legislative success" in terms of committee action—whether a bill receives a markup hearing and how often groups testify before congressional hearings. I do so for a number of reasons, the first being that civil rights groups themselves believe that committee action in their preferred direction is a crucial first step toward achieving their goals. Committee markup sessions give members an opportunity to modify a bill and to add provisions before they pass it out of committee. Committee markups are widely used in the House; they are less common in the Senate, whose limited membership makes markup sessions less necessary.

From hearings, lawmakers obtain valuable information that helps them craft a bill or determine whether federal legislation is even needed to address a specific policy issue. Members of the public as well as representatives of advocacy groups testify before congressional committees about the possible benefits or effects of proposed bills (Baumgartner and Jones 1993; Jones and Baumgartner 2005; Hall 1996; Minta 2011; Minta and Sinclair-Chapman 2013; Schiller 2000; Sulkin 2005). Testifying at hearings ranked as one of the most valuable tools used by citizen groups to advocate for their interests before Congress. Testifying at hearings is not reserved only for interest groups; members of Congress often testify at hearings. Given that civil rights groups rely on black and Latino legislators to advocate for their interests, committee hearings testimony provides another layer of advocacy for their interests.

Plan of the Book

The chapters that follow explore the advocacy efforts and effectiveness of strategies used by minority civil rights groups and their legislative advocates to advance the policy interests of racial and ethnic minorities in Congress. Chapter 2 examines the historical advocacy efforts of black and Latino organizations to obtain civil rights. Specifically, I focus on how these minority interest groups have attempted to influence the federal governmental agenda, as well as where black and Latino groups have worked together and where they have opposed each other. The chapter considers efforts by minority groups to create advocates, highlighting how legislator diversity is an important part of their strategy—and particularly how they have focused on creating majority-minority districts to increase the likelihood of electing legislators more sympathetic to their agendas. The chapter also addresses how legislators grant access to civil rights organizations and the specific mechanism of access that operates between minority civil rights groups and minority legislators. Finally, the chapter discusses the limitations that citizen groups such as civil rights organizations face in gaining access to legislative allies, as well as the limitations of the strategy of creating majority-minority districts to improve representation.

Chapter 3 uses survey data on minority opinions regarding public policy issues to examine to what extent the legislative priorities and activities of minority civil rights organizations and minority legislators have represented the interests of blacks and Latinos from the mid-1970s through the late 2000s. Has the correspondence between minority preferences and legislators' activity changed or remained the same during this time? Does the organizational capacity of organizations affect how effective groups are in attending to their constituents' interests? Additionally, I examine whether the funding sources of civil rights organizations play a role in determining which issues they address the most. Specifically, does the increasing reliance of groups on corporate and private foundation funding affect the level of attention groups dedicate to black and Latino interests?

Chapter 4 begins this study's systematic analysis of the extent to which committee diversity in the House was important to the legislative success of civil rights organizations. Specifically, do minority organizations achieve greater policy success because there are more Black and Latino legislators in Congress? Although civil rights groups are criticized for their failure and inaction on various policy issues, little is known about whether the legislative strategy of these groups has resulted in the systematic success or failure of their policy interests. As a result of the political realignment of the political parties in the late 1960s, the Democratic Party has been more associated with advancing the interests of blacks and Latinos than the Republican Party (Carmines and Stimson 1989). Consequently, I examined the lobbying activity for civil rights groups when the Democratic Party controlled the House and the legislative agenda. The 110th and 111th Congresses were selected because they permit an examination of the legislative success that civil rights organizations experienced under changing partisan control of the presidency. Specifically, are groups likely to be more successful in getting committee action on their bills when Democrats control both the House and Senate? These congresses provide leverage in measuring the legislative success of civil rights groups, as well as the potential effects, if any, of having a divided versus a unified government.[7]

Chapter 5 examines witness testimony as a form of political advocacy and legislative success for black and Latino civil rights organizations and their legislative advocates. Testifying at committee hearings is an important tool that advocacy groups use to represent their constituent interests on legislation before congressional committees. I examine whether the presence of more black and Latino legislators in Congress leads to greater opportunities for minority civil rights groups to testify before House committees in the twenty-first century than there were in the 1950s, as well as whether black and Latino legislators testify more frequently and, as a result, supplement the groups' efforts. What role did they play, if any, in changing the focus of the political environment?

I conclude in chapter 6 by discussing the strengths and weaknesses of greater participation by minority civil rights groups in the pressure group system, focusing on whether the reliance on minority legislators as advocates is the best path to achieve progressive policy change—especially in an era of congressional polarization in which significant legal efforts are under way to weaken the provisions of the Voting Rights Act. Finally, I offer some thoughts on whether movements such as Black Lives Matter and #MeToo are reasonable alternatives for bringing about policy change for minorities.

TWO

A History of Black and Latino Interest Group Advocacy in the United States

In the *Federalist Papers*, James Madison and Alexander Hamilton argued that pluralism, along with frequent elections and the separation of powers, would limit the ability of factions to acquire a monopoly on governmental power that could be used to oppress the minority. For pluralism to work effectively, the Federalists envisioned a diverse society in which all groups would be represented. These competing groups of citizens would have the opportunity to lobby the government for redress if one group became too powerful or even tyrannical (Truman 1971).

Although the pluralist ideal is admirable, pluralism in practice fails to operate when all groups in society are not represented adequately or equally. Although racial and ethnic minorities were not initially envisioned as having membership in American pluralist society, blacks and Latinos and the organizations representing their interests have fought to gain inclusion in American civil society. In the early 1900s, blacks in coalition with liberal whites formed the National Association for the Advancement of Colored People and the National Urban League to advocate for black interests, while Mexican Americans formed the League of United Latin American Citizens to represent the interests of Latinos (Marquez 1993; Sullivan 2009; Weiss 1974). Like many other organized interest groups, these civil rights groups worked actively to get Congress to address issues that affected the interests of their members. Their staff lobbied and testified before congressional committees in an attempt to get the federal government to protect the civil and political rights of blacks and Latinos. Unlike many other interest groups, however, minority civil rights organizations were disadvantaged because Jim Crow laws effectively disenfranchised blacks and Latinos. While civil rights organizations achieved some success, it was not until the civil rights movement and Chicano movement of the 1950s and 1960s that they increased their political influence within Congress.

With the passage of the Civil Rights Act and the Voting Rights Act, barriers to minority political participation such as literacy tests, grandfather clauses, and poll taxes were eliminated. Civil rights leaders argued that white politicians could no longer ignore minority interests and had to be responsive to the needs of the minority community (Davidson and Grofman 1994; Guinier 1994). Despite minorities gaining the right to vote, white Southern Democrats and some Northern Democrats refused to act on policy issues important to minority civil rights organizations and minority interests (Zelizer 2004). Dissatisfied with Congress's lack of responsiveness to the civil rights agenda and with continued efforts by Southerners to dilute minority voting power, minority civil rights groups formed a coalition with the American Civil Liberties Union to advocate for the creation of majority-minority districts (Davidson and Grofman 1994). They argued that blacks and Latinos had the right to elect a candidate of their choice, and they believed black and Latino legislators would be more responsive to minority interests than white legislators were.

This chapter examines the historical legislative advocacy efforts of black and Latino civil rights organizations to get Congress to support minority policy interests, with attention first to efforts by civil rights leaders to have an impact on the legislative process in the period before black and Latino civil and political rights were reaffirmed by the Civil Rights Act and the Voting Rights Act. I examine the policies these groups pursued, who their legislative advocates were, and how successful they were in their advocacy efforts. Turning to the period after blacks and Latinos were formally incorporated in pluralist governance, or after the VRA, I examine whether advocacy groups used similar tactics to those they had used in the previous era, as well as whether they had access to a greater variety of legislators to push their agendas. Although in this period minorities had voting power that politicians had to respect, minority voting alone did not necessarily make white legislators more responsive to the policy needs of civil rights organizations. Black and Latino legislators were more responsive to the policy needs of civil rights organizations, both before and after the passage of the Voting Rights Act. Civil rights organizations engaged in litigation through the redistricting process to increase the number of black and Latino legislators. The chapter concludes with an analysis of the efficacy of this strategy, as well as some of its limitations.

History of Black Civil Rights Advocacy

Advocacy efforts for black civil rights have been extensively documented (see, e.g., McAdam 1982; Morris 1984). The NAACP, NUL, and LCCR have been the most active and consistent organizations in national advocacy for civil rights for blacks.[1] These groups were established to improve the social, political, and economic conditions of blacks, but they had different objectives and used different strategies to achieve their missions. The NAACP was founded in 1909 to advocate for the political and civil rights of people of color in the United States, but most specifically for blacks. The NUL was founded in 1910 and was designed to provide social services to blacks who lived in urban areas. As a result, the NAACP performed more political advocacy while the NUL focused on raising money to fund the provision of social services, as well as on negotiating with privately with businesses (Weiss 1974). The NUL switched its focus from behind-the-scenes bargaining to pressure politics with the onset of the Great Depression and the New Deal era of the 1930s.[2] Both the NAACP and the NUL lobbied to ensure that blacks were included in the provisions of the programs that were designed to bring the nation out of its economic crisis.

Civil Rights Advocacy, 1910s to 1940s

The NAACP was established during a period of considerable racial violence, when black Americans' political rights and enfranchisement were being drastically curtailed. Moderates such as Booker T. Washington argued that blacks should focus on economic empowerment and that civil and political rights should come later. Many of the founders of the NAACP were appalled by the unchecked white mob violence against blacks, however, and argued for federal intervention to protect blacks and provide the justice that state and local courts would not. Given the nationwide prevalence of lynching, the NAACP spent most of its energy in its early decades focused on getting the federal government to stop the lynching of blacks by white mobs. An analysis of NAACP board meeting minutes from 1909–1921 shows that the NAACP spent significant time on criminal justice issues, primarily antilynching legislation (Francis 2014). The NAACP passed resolutions at its annual convention and directed its lobbyist James Weldon Johnson to focus primarily on lobbying Congress and the president on behalf of antilynching legislation.

What is instructive about the antilynching fight is the considerable success of the insider lobbying done by Johnson and legislators who decided to support the NAACP's efforts. From 1900 to 1940, more than two hundred antilynching bills were introduced in Congress.[3] The House and Senate held twelve hearings on lynching.[4] The House passed three of the antilynching measures, but all these bills failed to pass in the Senate. The main sponsor of antilynching legislation in the House was Congressman Leonidas Dyer (R-MO). Dyer was a liberal white Republican who represented a district that included St. Louis, Missouri. In supporting this minority issue, however, Dyer was the exception and not the rule. In fact, he sponsored various legislation supported by blacks. Examination of his ideology scores shows that he was generally more liberal than other Northern legislators.[5] His specific reasons for supporting the fight against lynching are unclear. Although there was a growing black population in St. Louis, these voters were effectively disenfranchised and therefore did not affect his electoral chances. There was a major race riot in East St. Louis, Illinois, directly across the Mississippi River from his district, that might have affected his beliefs regarding civil rights (Francis 2014). Whatever the reason, Dyer was a strong legislative ally for the NAACP and the primary contact for James Weldon Johnson and Walter White, the NAACP's assistant secretary.

The NAACP's push for antilynching laws did not succeed, but the organization did not abandon its legislative strategy—it did shift most of its resources to obtaining minority civil rights through the federal judiciary. The switch to this legal strategy was pursued only once it became apparent that the Senate, dominated by Southern Democrats, would not allow antilynching legislation to pass (Francis 2014).

Although the National Urban League supported antilynching legislation, the group did not participate extensively in federal advocacy on this issue. In 1934, the NUL sent Elmer Carter, editor of the organization's magazine, to testify at the Senate hearing on antilynching, but most of the work done on the issue was done by the NAACP (Weiss 1974).

If legislators are motivated primarily by strategic factors, such as the desire to be reelected and constituency influence, then why were the NAACP and NUL able to gain access to members of Congress in the first half of the twentieth century? Even though blacks had growing political power in Northern urban areas, there was not a strong electoral incentive for legislators to advocate for or support issues favored by minority interest groups. During the antilynching campaign, most Democrats and Republicans did not engage actively in the debates. And yet, despite the fact that there were few minority representatives in the House, the NAACP effected considerable movement on federal antilynching legislation in Congress. Party considerations played a role: the GOP was still the "Party of Lincoln" and a reluctant supporter of civil rights for blacks. When the Republican Party regained control of both chambers of Congress, it passed antilynching legislation in the House. This partial victory represented the lobbying strength of the NAACP on the issue. Although the Senate's refusal to pass Dyer's bill was considered a failure, lynching did decrease across the United States as a result of both congressional action and the advocacy efforts of the antilynching coalition led by Ida B. Wells and the NAACP (Francis 2014).

From 1930 to 1950, civil rights bills were sponsored mainly by white legislators from New York, where the NAACP and NUL had headquarters, such as Senator Wagner, and by black members of Congress. The influx of blacks into the urban politics machine in New York helped sway these members to provide access to minority civil rights groups and support civil rights legislation (Hamilton 1991). The NAACP gave up hope of passing antilynching legislation. Its congressional allies—still white Northern liberals—continued to forward bills that received hearings but failed to become law.

Advocacy for Economic Relief and Social Welfare

The efforts of the NAACP and the NUL to get Congress to include blacks in New Deal policies and fight racial discrimination in New Deal programs are well chronicled (Brown 1999; Weiss 1974). The NAACP and the NUL devoted significant time to ensuring that blacks had access to work relief and social welfare programs. The NUL produced reports and studies showing how blacks were disproportionately affected by unemployment. Representatives of the NUL and NAACP testified at hearings documenting how white administrators were not providing program benefits to blacks. When the Social Security Act was debated before congressional committees, the NUL and NAACP testified that the exclusion of domestic and agricultural workers from Social Security discriminated against blacks. Congress ultimately refused to include these categories of workers because blacks and Latinos were more likely to hold these jobs.[6] The sponsor of the bill did not want to include these employment categories for fear their inclusion might upset southern legislators who held leadership positions on powerful congressional committees.

The NUL also took on a major role in pushing to have blacks included in the collective-bargaining protections granted to labor under the Wagner Act. The NUL's position was that the act should include provisions that barred labor unions from discriminating against blacks. Representatives of the NUL met several times with Sen. Robert Wagner (D-NY) in order to encourage him to include the protections in his bill. He did not include them, however, again for fear of losing Southern support.

Black Legislative Advocates

Before the civil rights movement of the 1950s and 1960s, black civil rights organizations relied heavily on black legislators to represent their interests. When the House added two black legislators—among them Oscar DePriest (R-IL), the first black person elected to Congress since 1901—these legislators sponsored a variety of New Deal legislation that favored black interests. Black legislators included DePriest, Rep. Arthur Mitchell (D-IL), Rep. William Dawson (D-IL), and Rep. Adam Clayton Powell (D-NY), the latter of whom became the most well known and outspoken advocate for civil rights for blacks. The NAACP could reliably depend on Powell to represent its interests in Congress. In the 1950s, Powell introduced many civil rights bills and amendments, including amendments to eliminate segregation in public accommodations, housing, and employment (the so-called Powell Amendments). According to one account, "The organization [the NAACP] was the quarterback that threw the ball to Powell, who, to his credit, was more than happy to catch and run with it" (Hamilton 1991, 227). Powell sponsored civil rights legislation more frequently than did white legislators. His voting record scorecards matched the interests of black civil rights organizations. Powell provided this level of support to blacks even though the NAACP was a nonprofit organization and could not donate funds to his campaigns. Powell was the champion for civil rights that Rep. Arthur Mitchell (D-IL) did not want to be. Mitchell was connected to the Chicago political machine and thus prioritized district concerns over the interests of representing a national black constituency.

When lobbying disclosure laws were under consideration to provide greater transparency to the public regarding how much groups were spending on lobbying, civil rights groups such as the NAACP opposed them on the basis that they would be used to curtail the NAACP's advocacy activities. Correspondence between Thurgood Marshall and Leslie Perry from the 1940s reveals the nature of NAACP officials' concerns. In the 1950s, after the NAACP was victorious in *Brown v. Board of Education*, many segregationists wanted the IRS to evaluate the lobbying activities of the NAACP, claiming that it violated the lobbying regulations imposed on 501(c)(3) organizations. White supremacist groups also wanted the membership lists of the NAACP in order to target individual members with harassment.

Again in the 1970s, NAACP resolutions opposed changes to lobbying disclosure laws on the basis that they would limit the advocacy efforts of organizations.

By then, the NAACP had made significant gains that it wanted to protect. The civil rights movement of the 1950s and 1960s had allowed civil rights organizations to increase their influence in the legislative arena. The result was the passage of the Civil Rights Act in 1964 and the Voting Rights Act in 1965. The NAACP lobbyist Clarence Mitchell, who drafted the bills that became the Civil Rights Act and Voting Rights Act, had access to many advocates who supported civil rights legislation, including Adam Clayton Powell Jr. In the 1970s, the brother of Clarence Mitchell, U.S. House Rep. Parren Mitchell (D-MD), was elected to Congress. He helped found the CBC and was a champion for civil rights.

The increasing political power of blacks improved the bargaining strength of the NAACP, but the number of minority legislators remained small in the 1960s compared to their proportion of the overall population, and the NAACP continued to struggle to get Congress to pay attention to civil rights legislation. Nonetheless, in the aggregate, the NAACP had great success in getting Congress to pass federal legislation that protected the civil rights of blacks, including their right to vote.

By the 1970s, black Americans were fully incorporated into the political system. The reluctance of white Democrats to support the NAACP's civil rights agenda and replicate the success they had with black legislators influenced the organization's decision to spearhead efforts to increase the number of black legislators in Congress and in state and local lawmaking bodies. Racial redistricting would be the tool used by black civil rights organizations to achieve that goal.

History of Latino Civil Rights Advocacy

Latinos have been represented as a faction agitating for consideration from the legislature since the early 1900s, but the struggle to establish civil rights for Latinos did not follow the same trajectory as it did for black Americans. Before the 1970s, in fact, Latinos were not recognized as a minority group by the U.S. Census Bureau or other federal agencies. Although Latinos were not explicitly addressed in formal segregation laws based on the "separate but equal" doctrine established by *Plessy v. Ferguson* or in the South's Jim Crow restrictions that barred blacks from civil and political life, they experienced much of the same discriminatory treatment as blacks, especially in the Southwest. Mexican Americans could not serve on juries, were restricted from voting, and were barred from attending schools and making use of public accommodations used by Anglos (Behnken 2011; Kaplowitz 2005). Discrimination against Latinos in housing and employment likewise limited their ability to thrive as citizens. They were restricted to mostly low-wage jobs in the service industry and agriculture. Discriminatory housing and lending laws led Latinos to live in segregated communities and in substandard housing.

Civil Rights Advocacy, 1930–1960s

Several advocacy groups were established to fight for the civil rights of Mexican Americans, including the League of United Latin American Citizens in 1929 and the American GI Forum in 1948. The extent to which these organizations were effective has been contested by historians and other scholars influenced by the Chicano movement. Although Latinos experienced much of the same discrimination as blacks in housing, labor markets, and public accommodations from the 1920s through the 1950s, LULAC, the largest and most prominent Latino rights organization, pursued an assimilationist strategy and did not call for civil rights legislation to protect Mexican Americans as a racialized minority. Instead, LULAC officials argued that Mexican Americans should receive equal treatment under existing laws because they were "white" citizens (Kaplowitz 2005; Marquez 1993). In an effort to fully assimilate to an "American" identity, LULAC even supported immigration policies such as Operation Wetback, which deported undocumented Mexican workers and even some Mexican Americans (Garcia Bedolla 2009; Kaplowitz 2005; Marquez 1993). Unlike the NAACP, LULAC did not spend much time lobbying Congress to pass civil rights legislation. LULAC officials preferred to pursue informal negotiations at the local level and, if necessary, to apply local pressure (Behnken 2011). The group also engaged in litigation to bring about change, but its limited resources made this a rare strategy. During the group's early years, LULAC focused on education, particularly the integration of schools. Its desegregation efforts centered on integrating Mexican Americans with Anglos, but not with blacks.

Indeed, during the civil rights movement, LULAC refused to work with black civil rights groups to gain civil rights protections for minorities. While LULAC leaders' refusal to work with blacks might have been a result of racist attitudes against blacks, it might have had more to do with secondary marginalization than with antipathy toward blacks (Cohen 1999; Kim 2000). That is, LULAC feared that the association between Latinos and a similarly marginalized group such as blacks would diminish Latinos' chances of receiving equal treatment from whites. The unwillingness of LULAC and the American GI Forum to work with black advocacy groups frustrated black leaders. Clarence Mitchell expressed his disappointment with the lack of support received from LULAC and the GI Forum for civil rights legislation (Watson 1990). LULAC officials did not join the LCCR—a leadership group that represented all civil rights minorities, formed in 1950—arguing that their struggle differed from that of blacks and that they wanted to remain separate.

It was LULAC's assimilationist, separatist approach to civil rights that caused political scientist Ben Marquez to state that the group did little to improve civil rights for minorities (1993). Although LULAC did not join the civil rights movement, it did inspire ethnic-group consciousness among Mexican Americans. Many Mexican Americans did not agree with LULAC's stance on civil rights protections. The rise of the Chicano movement forced LULAC to reconsider its long-held assimilationist strategy and pushed the group to support efforts by Mexican Americans, along with other Spanish-speaking groups, to form a pan-ethnic identity. In response, LULAC began to pursue a strategy recognizing that Mexican Americans needed federal laws to protect their distinct needs and to devote resources to lobbying the executive branch for benefits; it gave less time to lobbying Congress.

As LULAC was making this shift, several new Latino civil rights organizations were forming in the 1960s. The Southwest Council of La Raza and the Mexican American Legal Defense and Educational Fund (modeled after the NAACP's Legal Defense Fund) were both established in 1968 to advocate for the broad interests of Mexican Americans. The Southwest Council of La Raza, in an attempt to address the needs of all Latinos, changed its name to the National Council of La Raza (NCLR). The name change signaled the group's decision to move away from its identity as a regional group that focused only on the issues of Mexican Americans.[7] This shift was important, because black interest groups were perceived as national groups, and as such, they garnered a larger share of federal resources and attention. Latino interest groups were similarly interested in gaining more attention and resources (Mora 2014). The NCLR and other Latino-focused groups lobbied Congress and the U.S. Census Bureau to create the pan-ethnic designation "Hispanic" to describe Spanish-speaking Americans. The creation of this designation marked a definitive break with LULAC and the GI Forum's assimilationism, establishing Latino Americans as a separate group eligible to receive federal protections and resources. Still, the NAACP and other black advocacy groups remained hesitant to collaborate with the new Latino advocacy groups because of Latino organizations' history of refusing to support civil rights for blacks (Behnken 2011; Kaplowitz 2005).

By the 1970s, the NCLR, LULAC, and MALDEF had established offices in Washington, DC, to advocate for Latino issues. Lobbying Congress was not a new activity for the NCLR and MALDEF, but for LULAC it marked a major shift; most of LULAC's advocacy prior to the 1960s had focused on contacting and lobbying presidents directly (Kaplowitz 2005). The Latino advocacy groups focused much of their work on establishing language provisions for Spanish-speaking Americans. The NCLR's primary function was to provide funding for its community service organizations and affiliates.

Latino Legislative Advocates

In terms of legislative advocates, Latino groups were most successful in finding white liberals to support their goals. Early defenders of Latino civil rights included legislators Edward Roybal (D-CA) and Henry B. Gonzalez (D-TX). Although Latino groups pushed for action on bilingual education and immigration reform for many years, few legislators would sponsor these bills. In the 1950s and 1960s, the Southern conservative James Eastland (D-MS) refused to hold a hearing on immigration (Tichenor 2002).

Wong (2006) has found, however, that Latino groups exerted influence on immigration policy long before their constituents became electorally powerful. She argues that ethnic organizations were successful because they practiced an inclusive form of identity politics, casting their demands for rights in universal terms. Latino organizations, like Asian American civil rights groups, built a broad coalition, forming alliances with other civil rights groups and humanitarian organizations. This coalition helped them sway the votes of moderate and undecided lawmakers.[8]

The Push for Majority-Minority Districts

The passage of the Voting Rights Act in 1965 dramatically changed the political context in the United States for minority advocacy in Congress. Minority citizens who had been disenfranchised and restricted from participating in formal politics were now included. This was especially true in the South. Laws established during the Jim Crow era to disenfranchise blacks, such as literacy tests and white primaries, were eliminated by the VRA. The Twenty-Fourth Amendment eliminated the poll tax. These measures formally eradicated the barriers that had limited the ability of blacks and other minorities to participate in the political process. Prior to the passage of the VRA, only 15 percent of blacks in Mississippi were registered to vote; after the passage of the new law, more than 60 percent were registered to vote (Grofman, Handley, and Niemi 1992). Black representation provided additional leverage for civil rights organizations, which could demonstrate to legislators that minority organizations represented a constituency that could affect legislators' electoral chances.

Many organizations argued that improved minority access to the franchise did not necessarily make white legislators more responsive to minority interests. Although blacks represented a significant share of voters in many legislators' districts or states, the voting dilution efforts of white Southerners diminished the electoral power of blacks. As a result, white legislators refused to address issues favored by minority organizations and their membership. So, while the VRA eliminated the harsh rhetoric used by Southern legislators and stopped anti–civil rights bills from being introduced by Southern segregationists such as James Eastland (D-MS) and Richard Russell (D-MS), in a substantive sense white Democrats did not actively represent the interests of black voters.

Voting scores kept by the LCCR from the 95th Congress (1977–1978) confirm that there were significant differences in support for black-supported legislation among congressional Democrats (see table 2.1). Not surprisingly, black Democrats were the most supportive of the LCCR's civil rights agenda, and white Republicans were the least supportive. Black Democrats scored 94 percent, while white Democrats scored 68 percent and Republicans, 28 percent. Civil rights activists argued that white Southern Democrats could ignore the interests of blacks because of racially polarized voting: white Democrats still comprised the majority of most districts, and white legislators were fearful they would hurt their chances of reelection if they supported civil rights legislation. Even in areas outside the South, where white Democrats were more liberal, white legislators were not as responsive to minority

Table 2.1.   LCCR Legislators' Vote Scores, 95th Congress (1977–1978)

Party and race/ethnicity (region)	Report-card score
Black Democrats	94%
White Democrats	68%
White Democrats (Southern)	44%
White Democrats (Not Southern)	80%
White Republicans	28%
White Southern Republicans	12%
Asian	92%
Latino	68%

issues as were minority legislators. Black legislators scored 94 percent, while white Democrats from outside the South scored 80 percent.

Not only did white legislators refuse to vote as civil rights organizations would have preferred; they also sponsored less civil rights legislation than black legislators. In the 95th Congress, white Democrats sponsored an average of 0.79 civil rights bills, compared to 1.25 for black legislators. White Southern Democrats were largely responsible for the lower rate for white Democrats, with Democrats from the South sponsoring only 0.067 of civil rights bills.[9]

Frustrated by the reluctance of white legislators to support their interests, the representatives of civil rights organizations believed that increasing the number of minorities in Congress would benefit their advocacy efforts. As Guinier (1994, 43) points out, "The perception that blacks were not effectively represented in majority-white jurisdictions because of racially polarized voting formed the basis of the litigation strategy." More advocates would mean more entry points into the legislative system.[10] It would also enable the creation of winning coalitions for policies promoted by organizations with relatively scarce resources. Minority legislators in Congress could advocate as much as they wanted for civil rights groups without being constrained by lobbying disclosure laws.

The primary way that civil rights organizations worked to increase minority membership in Congress involved lawsuits filed under the VRA in an attempt to create majority-black and majority-Latino state legislative and congressional districts. Throughout the country, the NAACP, MALDEF, and the ACLU won a number of U.S. Supreme Court decisions to create majority-minority districts from the 1970s through the 1990s. The courts ruled that multimember congressional districts hindered the ability of blacks to win elected office. The elimination of multimember districts and the establishment of single-member districts helped increase the number of majority-black and majority-Latino districts. Section 5 of the VRA permits the U.S. Department of Justice to perform "preclearance," that is, to review the redistricting plans of states that have a history of violating the voting rights of blacks and Latinos—usually Southern states. The Justice Department, as well as the courts, ruled that if states had an opportunity to create majority-black or majority-Latino districts, then they were compelled to do so. Although opponents of majority-minority districts have argued that these districts are unconstitutional and do not benefit minorities (Swain 1993; Thernstrom 1987), majority-minority districts have increased minority representation in state legislatures and the U.S. Congress.

Minority organizations' leadership believed that redistricting would

Table 2.2.   Black and Latino Legislators in the House after Redistricting Years (1971–2011)

Census year	Number of black legislators	Number of Latino legislators
1971	12	5
1981	18	7
1991	27	11
2001	37	19
2011	40	27

bring even more black and Latino legislators to Congress who would be strong advocates for their organizations' policy issues. The presence of minority legislators would also give the groups greater access to legislators. Redistricting produced the infusion of minority legislators that civil rights groups had hoped for. Table 2.2 shows the number of black and Latino legislators in the House after a redistricting cycle.

In 1971, there were only twelve African American members and five Latinos in Congress, but by 2011, forty African American and twenty-seven Latino members were serving in Congress. The influence of the civil rights movement was apparent. Minority legislators organized into caucuses with the express purpose of lobbying for the interests of minorities, not just in their own districts but also nationally. These minority legislators formed the Congressional Black Caucus in 1971 and the Congressional Hispanic Caucus in 1976. The CBC and CHC have expanded their capacity to advocate for minority interests inside and outside of Congress by establishing an array of nonprofit organizations. The CBC created the CBC Foundation, the CBC Policy and Leadership Institute, and the CBC Political Action Committee to assist in advocacy on African American issues. Similarly, the CHC launched the CHC Foundation and the CHC Institute to advocate for Latino issues. These entities allow caucus members to gather information on policy preferences directly from black and Latino voters, as well as from large and small civil rights organizations. The CBC and CHC foundations, for example, sponsor annual legislative weekends. These weekends allow constituents to meet with legislators and their staff to discuss issues that are important to the black and Latino communities.

How Diversity Improves Lobbying Policy Success

The new minority members of Congress had to decide whether they were civil rights activists or legislators. This debate is recounted by Rep. Louis Stokes (D-OH):

The taskforce came back with a report in which they said to us we were too limited to be all things to all black people in America. They also said to us that we had to understand our role as legislators: that we were not civil rights leaders, that we were legislators elected to the Congress in order to enact legislation that betters the conditions of black people and minorities all over this country. So to that end, one of things that we recommended was that we spread ourselves out among the committee system of the house. We had to utilize our small number to do what we could in the committee system. (C-SPAN 2009)

That is, after an exhaustive debate, the new minority legislators determined that they would be legislators first—but their strong connections to minority rights organizations is undeniable. The NUL stated in its papers that the CBC was a valuable resource through which the NUL would aim to work in Congress. Black legislators believed they had a responsibility to help address the needs of all blacks. Many felt they had a more legitimate claim to represent the interests of blacks than did even the civil rights groups, because they were elected representatives.

As Bauer, Pool, and Dexter (1963) have argued, minority interest groups might be nothing more than service bureaus for legislators' intentions. The fact that legislators are constrained by resources and the amount of time they have to spend on any single issue gives interest groups power, because legislators rely on them to provide the information they need to reduce electoral uncertainty (Hall and Deardorff 2006; Hansen 1991). It remains an open question, then, whether minority interest groups are indeed able to exert influence on the behavior of members of Congress or whether they are simply providing information and lobbying their "friends" to take actions that those legislators would have taken regardless.

Standard strategic explanations for legislator behavior omit to account for the influence of racial and ethnic group consciousness, however. Minority civil rights organizations value the advocacy efforts of black and Latino legislators and consider these legislators a vital part of their coalition. The NUL, NCLR, and NAACP make this opinion clear in their official documents and minutes. Minority legislators and minority civil rights groups are not always on the same page, of course, despite their common interests. Although black and Latino civil rights organizations openly disagreed on including language provisions in the VRA, for example, CBC members broke with the preference of the NAACP's Washington Bureau lobbyist Clarence Mitchell and supported the provisions. Still, studies of political representation demonstrate that minority legislators are more likely to support minority-interest legislation than are white legislators, regardless of political party and the size of the black or Latino voting-age populations in their districts. The voting scorecards used by civil rights groups show that minority Democratic legislators are closely aligned to the groups' policy preferences. Interest groups are more likely to lobby their allies, and so civil rights groups are more likely to lobby Democrats, especially minority Democrats. DW-NOMINATE scores, commonly used to assess legislators' ideological preferences on a liberal-conservative scale, where −1 is very liberal and 1 is very conservative. The scores show that minority legislators are more liberal on issues that are most important to civil rights organizations.[11]

Minority organizations also have access to minority legislators because many of these legislators come from the ranks of the civil rights organizations themselves. Legislators need credible information from groups that will help them make the correct policy choices and aid their reelection efforts (Hansen 1991). Minority legislators establish relationships with minority interest groups and their leaders because many of these minority legislators were once active members of the same organizations. Before he was elected to Congress, for example, Rep. William Clay (D-MO) engaged in many protests and was a member of the NAACP Youth Council. Latino legislators were similarly active members of organizations such as the NCLR and LULAC (Martinez 2009). Rep. Ed Pastor (D-AZ) served as secretary of the NCLR in the 1970s before his election to Congress.

That minority legislators and civil rights organizations are interrelated is not a new observation. Minta (2011) demonstrated that a significant number of minority legislators, as compared to white legislators, were members of civil rights organizations. What is important here is that the interrelationship between minority legislators and civil rights organizations means that they have similar policy preferences. Because interest groups usually lobby their friends, this helps foster access. Minority legislators might be more willing to provide this access even without having received PAC contributions from civil rights organizations. In an interview, Luis Torres of LULAC stated that when there are more Latino members in Congress, they can provide access to LULAC on even minor issues, such as reserving meeting rooms and other work space.[12] Legislators who share a worldview with civil rights organization staff are more willing to assist.

Not only have civil rights organizations developed a relationship of trust with minority legislators, but many of these legislators also helped create the districts they now serve. Congressman Louis Stokes (D-OH), the first black House member from Ohio and the brother of Carl Stokes, was the head of the NAACP committee that filed a lawsuit that created Ohio's first majority-black district. Louis Stokes recalls:

> Ohio had never had a Black in the U.S. Congress, and there were people who intended that it would not occur, so they gerrymandered the 21st Congressional district in such a way that they completely diluted the black population, and so there was not basic strength in that congressional district. Carl [Stokes] came home from Columbus, OH, and went to the NAACP and asked them to file a lawsuit against the legislature he was serving in which had gerrymandered his district. I was the NAACP's Legal Redress Committee Chairman. So as a result of it, they gave me the case for me and my committee to handle. So we took the case, we filed a lawsuit on his behalf, and it took three years for the case to come up in court. (Brown, Minta, and Sinclair-Chapman 2016, 153)

Carl Stokes later left the state legislature and became the first black mayor of Cleveland, Ohio, while Louis Stokes ran for and won the House seat that he helped create.

In general, minority interest groups and minority legislators agreed on the importance of state legislatures' redrawing district lines to increase the number of majority-minority districts in Congress. For many black and Latino state legislators, a majority-minority district offered an opportunity to win a higher political office, especially in the South. Although the creation of these districts offered mutually beneficial opportunities for minority interest groups and legislators, there were disagreements between the interest groups and minority legislators over the number of majority-minority districts that should be created. The NAACP, MALDEF, and ACLU wanted to create as many minority districts as was feasibly possible, but minority legislators were not in favor of maximizing these districts if it would cost white Democratic incumbents. This was especially true in the 1990s in Virginia and North Carolina (Grofman 1998). Minority legislators knew the value of serving in a Congress where Democrats held the majority of seats. Thus, reports about the black Democrats working with Republicans, or the so-called unholy alliance to create majority-minority districts, are vastly overstated and do not match the empirical data (Crayton 2002).

Access Points

If influence is about access to members, then the NAACP has achieved access in several ways. The CBC Institute was established by the CBC to gain insight into policy issues from constituents and provide recommendations to members of Congress. The board of directors is comprised of Fortune 500 company members and representatives of other interest groups. Hilary Shelton, the lead lobbyist for the NAACP, serves on the CBC Political Education and Leadership Institute's board. In addition, the institute has a boot camp designed to train black Americans to run for elected office.

The CBC has a close relationship with civil rights groups. It was responsible for helping to create TransAfrica, a major advocate for policies to end apartheid in South Africa. Rep. Charles Diggs (D-MI) was instrumental in the creation of this group. The CBC believed that insider and outsider advocacy would encourage the United States to take a tougher stance against the apartheid regime of South Africa (Tillery 2011).

How Diversity Works in the Legislative Process

Greater racial and ethnic diversity on committees allows minority legislators to act as gatekeepers. They can increase the likelihood that legislation supported by civil rights interest groups will receive committee action. They can also ensure that legislation that is not favorable to civil rights groups never makes it beyond the committee stage, thus using both the positive and the negative agenda power of committee members. Generally speaking, minority legislators are committed to the collective uplift of marginalized groups, especially racial and ethnic minorities and the poor—similar to civil rights organizations. The NAACP, NCLR, CBC, CHC, and Congressional Asian Pacific American Caucus (CAPAC) were founded on, and continue to possess, these same principles of racial group uplift.

CAPAC was established in the 1994 by Norman Mineta. In an interview with C-SPAN, he said that he had noticed the success of the CBC and CHC and realized that Asian Americans did not have a similar organization (C-SPAN 2012). So he spoke with the members of the CBC and CHC to figure how they were organized. Mineta then contacted Asian American legislators and reached out to the members of Congress who had a substantial number of Asian and Pacific Islander minorities in their districts.

Such groups balance legislators' reelection goals against the commitment legislators have to what I refer to as "strategic group uplift" (Minta 2011, 12–13). They work together through interethnic collaboration with umbrella groups such as the Congressional Tri-Caucus and the LCCR. The Working Group on Immigration is an example of civil rights groups working together to address an issue. The rising strength of the CBC and CHC has changed the fortunes of these groups, which once had to persuade reluctant Northern Democrats to sponsor their legislation when Southern Democrats would stall civil rights legislation in committees—as well as economic and labor legislation—by refusing to hold hearings. The NAACP passed several resolutions in defense of black legislators such as Charles Diggs and Edward Brooke, whom they believed were unfairly targeted by their opponents because of their race. In its policy statements, the NUL clearly identified the CBC as partners and supporters of their legislative advocacy efforts.

Such partnerships began to bridge old divides between black and Latino groups, as well. Although their strategies and interests diverged in the past, LULAC joined the LCCR in the 1970s. The history of competition between black and Latino advocates faded away. While black and Latino civil rights organizations continue to work primarily on issues that affect their respective groups (Hero and Preuhs 2013), when there are common issues that affect both the black and the Latino communities, these groups work together to achieve common goals, and there is more commonality among their interests in the 2000s than there was in the 1960s. More important, these alliances and other, similar coalitions, both formal and informal, have played a central role in making the Democratic Party more responsive to civil rights issues.

Limitations of Redistricting and Minority Legislators as Tools to Increase Influence

Although civil rights organizations believed that pursuing redistricting would lead to legislative institutions that were more responsive to civil rights and/or minority interests, many critics on the ideological left and right have argued that the strategy is flawed. While majority-black and majority-Latino districts have increased the number of black and Latino legislators in Congress, these critics argue, the existence of these districts has also led to an increase in the number of Republicans elected to Congress (Cameron, Epstein, and O'Halloran 1996; Lublin 1997; Swain 1993). By concentrating reliably Democrat-voting black and Latino voters instead of spreading them around, the strategy creates corresponding districts that are mostly white and difficult for Democratic candidates to win. Consequently, the Republican Party has gained control of the House due to the racial redistricting strategy. The net effect is that racial redistricting does not advantage civil rights organizations and their members, because Republicans are generally less supportive of civil rights issues than Democrats. Swain (1993) argues that civil rights groups should abandon the strategy because white Democrats can support minority interests just as well as black Democrats can. Guinier (1994) maintains that the redistricting strategy is not true to the aims and goals of the civil rights movement. The increase of minority legislators leads only to tokenism, while black legislators have no power to enact real, substantive change in favor of minority interests. In *Concordance*, Katherine Tate does not dispute that minority legislators are more responsive to minority interests than white legislators, but she argues that black legislators have moderated their policy positions, thus limiting the quality of representation they provide to black interests. According to Tate, black legislators have done this to gain more influence in the Democratic Party, thus sometimes supporting conservative policies like welfare reform that are detrimental to the interests of minorities.

Similar concerns were expressed when the CHC was formed in 1976: many feared that the CHC would be captured by the Democratic Party and would not advocate for Latinos. By contrast, the president of the National Council of La Raza (now UnidosUS), Raul Yzaguirre, applauded the formation of the caucus. According to Yzaguirre, "The Hispanic Caucus is much more here and now. Members of Congress are our best spokesmen. If I say something it is not the same."[13] Yzaguirre suggests that, far from being co-opted by the Democratic Party, minority legislators are the best possible spokespeople for minority interests—so much so that they are the ideal advocates for advancing UnidosUS's agenda. And indeed, CBC and CHC policy objectives are closely aligned with minority preferences and the policy priorities of civil rights organizations. The NAACP, LCCR, and National Hispanic Leadership Agenda (NHLA) voting scores for CBC and CHC members show that they are more responsive to the policy preferences of minority civil rights organizations than are nonmembers. The NAACP promotes a liberal agenda, and members of the CBC are more likely than any other group of legislators to support this agenda. The CBC does not rank priorities, but bills sponsored by the CBC have been closely aligned with minority preferences. The CHC similarly pays significant attention to the issues raised by Latino advocacy groups. Black legislators are substantially in agreement with the NAACP, and this support sets them apart from other legislators. Latino members' voting preferences are likewise aligned with the policy priorities of minority civil rights organizations. The CHC, for instance, listed immigration as its top priority. The caucus lists a broad set of legislative priorities, with task forces devoted to addressing those issues.

The alignment of civil rights organizations with Democrats has resulted in a party that is more responsive to minority interests but a Congress that is more polarized. The party unity scores of white legislators and minority legislators are more similar in the 2000s than they were in the 1970s. Demographic shifts and the redistricting favored by minority civil rights organizations have brought more black and Latino legislators into the Democratic delegation. As the Democratic Party has become more responsive to these legislators, the Republican Party has grown less supportive of issues favored by civil rights organizations. When Democrats are in power to shape the policy agenda, black and Latino advocacy groups have great influence. Specifically, they have supported bills aimed at eliminating racial profiling and the death penalty and providing reparations for blacks, all of which were important legislative priorities for the NAACP.

Civil rights organizations have expansive policy agendas that include many items in common with the Democratic Party's policy priorities. Issues such as equal pay and reducing sentencing disparities were championed by the Democratic Party. The policy priorities of Democrats are not synonymous with those of civil rights organizations, however. The priorities of political parties are broader in scope than those of civil rights organizations, and civil rights organizations also possess more liberal policy agendas than that of the Democratic Party. The most significant point here is that Democratic Party leadership, under the influence of minority legislators and minority civil rights organizations, has come to embrace what were once considered fringe issues, including eliminating the sentencing disparities for possession of crack and powder cocaine. Tate (2014) argues that the CBC has become less radical over time, but the results cited earlier show that CBC legislators are more liberal than white legislators. White Democrats are also moving closer into alignment with the voting positions of the CBC. Although the CBC is made up of better team players in the 2000s than in the 1970s, the CBC has had a liberalizing impact on the policy preferences of the Democratic Party.

Blacks and Latinos are primarily Democrats and liberal, but the official policy priorities announced by the Democratic Party in the 110th Congress did not directly align with the priorities of civil rights organizations. The policy priorities of the CBC and CHC, however, closely mirrored the policy agenda of the Democratic Party. Black groups tend to focus on issues that are explicitly racial, such as racial profiling and affirmative action. Latino groups tend to focus on issues such as immigration and education. Interestingly, the focus of the groups on these issues have been stable and have not changed considerably over the years except perhaps in their ranking, where Latinos now rank immigration as more important than education. In the 1970s, there was a heavy focus on full employment, which it was hoped would dramatically help decrease high levels of unemployment within black communities. In 2011, the civil rights groups no longer pushed for full employment measures such as the Humphrey-Hawkins bill, but they supported an economic stimulus package designed to shore up struggling local economies by providing funding for new jobs.

Even though redistricting may not be the cause of the GOP's rise to power, it is true that since the significant increase in the number of majority-minority districts in 1992, Democrats have controlled the House only four times.[14] Not only does racial redistricting lead to GOP control of Congress, but it has led to a rise in political polarization. By concentrating minority districts into majority-minority districts, the strategy has created safe districts for Democrats and Republicans, with neither party willing to compromise on policy issues. However, although it is the case that party polarization has increased as the number of majority-minority districts, most empirical research finds that redistricting is not the primary cause for party polarization (McCarty, Poole, and Rosenthal 2006). Furthermore, empirical research demonstrates that minority legislators do a better job than white legislators of representing minority interests (Clark 2019; Juenke and Preuhs 2012; Whitby 1997; Wilson 2017).

GOP control and party polarization creates dilemmas for civil rights organizations, who might lose out regardless of what party controls the majority. If the GOP is the majority party, then it becomes difficult for civil rights organizations to get congressional attention for their policy and legislative priorities. When Democrats are in control of the Congress, they might be less likely to advocate for progressive policy because the party leadership is concerned with maintaining the party's majority status. Lee (2016) has shown that polarization and the unwillingness of both parties to work together on many issues is a result of their desire to control the House or Senate. In the chapters that follow, consideration of each of these points about the limitations of civil rights organizations' reliance on and close relationship with legislative advocates will be incorporated into the argument and, where possible, tested and analyzed in the quantitative results.

Conclusion

The ideal of pluralism proposed in the *Federalist Papers* envisioned an American society in which organized interests could ensure the adequate representation of all Americans by putting pressure on Congress for redress of grievances or to limit the excessive representation of the powerful. Civil rights groups organized to represent the interests of blacks and Latinos worked within this system from their inception—with some success. Before the civil rights movement, however, the high barriers to voting for minorities, particularly in the U.S. South, made it difficult, and often impossible, for these groups to achieve more than limited success. White legislators could ignore representing the interests of blacks and Latinos and the civil rights groups that represented them without any fear of electoral retribution at the ballot box. The passage of the VRA and the subsequent legal challenges increased the political power of minorities by protecting their right to vote. For the first time, civil rights groups advocated before Congress representing a constituency that had power to hold legislators accountable at the ballot box, and in this sense to activate the power promised by Madison and Jefferson's ideal of pluralism.

Despite the new political strength of civil rights organizations in the formal political system, these groups were disadvantaged when lobbying on the Hill. Federal law restricted their ability to contribute to legislators and placed limits on how much they could lobby—factors that can affect legislative success. To mitigate the effects of these disadvantages, civil rights groups pursued a redistricting strategy designed to increase number of black and Latino legislators in Congress. Historically, minority legislators had been effective advocates for civil rights organizations, voting and sponsoring legislation in accordance with the interests of civil rights organizations. Prior to redistricting, however, their numbers were extremely low, and their attention to minority interests necessarily remained focused around civil rights issues. The greater presence of black and Latino legislators in the House gave hope to civil rights organizations that these legislators would be strong advocates for minority interests in civil rights and other policy areas.

As we have seen, Tate (2014) argues that formal incorporation in the political system has resulted in black legislators pursuing a less radical agenda. They are less likely to be adversarial than they were in the 1960s, for example, because many black political leaders are elected leaders, not activists or ministers. The data in this chapter show, however, that although election pressure does diminish some of the outsider tendencies of activists, the greater incorporation of black people in American politics has led to substantive gains for minorities. Greater access to minority legislators, as well as districts that have a greater share of minorities, have given black voters stronger legislative advocates. This permits them to have their policy preferences heard. Because most minority advocacy groups do not have the same resources as business associations, the access afforded to them by having more like-minded legislators in Congress is immense. Civil rights organizations, by engaging in redistricting, have done much to improve their level of access. The following chapters explore the level of disadvantage that civil rights groups face in the pressure group system and to what extent the greater number of black and Latino legislators can compensate for their limited financial resources.

THREE

Civil Rights Groups

The Challenge to Remain Relevant and Representative

From 2012 to 2016, protests erupted across the United States over the deaths of young black boys and men at the hands of law enforcement officers. One of the most publicized incidents involved a white officer, Darren Wilson, killing eighteen-year-old Michael Brown of Ferguson, Missouri. Officer Wilson claimed he shot Brown because he believed his life was in danger, but witnesses testified that Brown was fleeing and was not armed. Saddened and outraged by police actions, local leaders and activists marched to protest what they considered a pattern of unjust shootings across the country and to raise awareness of racial profiling in minority communities. The protests were organized loosely but adopted the name Black Lives Matter, a growing movement that highlighted the disparate treatment of black Americans by law enforcement.

The protests brought new attention to long-standing problems with racial profiling and police brutality, issues usually addressed by civil rights advocacy groups such as the NAACP, the LCCR, and the Congressional Black Caucus. Indeed, many of the protestors argued that civil rights organizations were not devoting enough attention to solving these problems. The nation's oldest civil rights organization, the NAACP, received the bulk of the criticism. Despite the NAACP's history of advocacy for black civil rights and economic justice, the organization is frequently criticized by liberal activists and scholars for not being courageous enough to solve the problems that black Americans face in the twenty-first century. Political scientist Melissa Harris-Perry argued this point in a May 2017 *New York Times* editorial: "Today, the N.A.A.C.P. carries the weight of history and burden of bureaucracy. But it does not seem willing to shed blood, literally, or in terms of the uncomfortable work that characterizes effective activism." Additionally, she stated that "the leaders may care about justice and fighting inequality, but they are consumed with organizational maintenance."[1] Harris-Perry argued that new groups such as the Black Youth Project 100, the Dream Defenders, and the Black Lives Matter Network were more effective in addressing black interests.

Civil rights organizations representing Latinos have met with similar criticism. According to political scientist Stella Rouse in a June 2017 article for NBC News, "The void in Latino national leadership is nothing new and perhaps not so surprising, given the diversity of group characteristics and group interests. However, in light of their ever increasing numbers, at a time when Latinos need a prominent and influential voice to promote their interests and oppose detrimental policies, the deficit in Latino leadership is all the more striking. Without individuals that can stand up against the current political environment, Latinos will likely continue to find themselves marginalized."[2] Rouse acknowledged that civil rights groups such as UnidosUS and LULAC exist, but she argued that they are not as prominent as groups organized on behalf of black Americans, and thus not as effective in advocating for Latino interests.

Harris-Perry's and Rouse's critiques of civil rights organizations are not new. Many scholars and liberal activists have argued that civil rights organizations do not effectively represent the interests of the younger generation of blacks and Latinos, or of the poor, of gays and lesbians, and of former prisoners. Cohen (1999) outlines how the NAACP, SCLC, and CBC have failed to adequately address the spread of the HIV/AIDS crisis in the black community because doing so would have meant advocating on behalf of doubly marginalized members of the community, namely, gay black men and intravenous drug users. The leaders of black civil rights organizations feared that proactively advocating for solutions for these subgroups would further reinforce and marginalize all black Americans. Similarly, Strolovitch (2007) found that minority and women's groups tend to focus on issues that benefit the most advantaged members of the group, such as the affluent, and place less focus on issues that would assist the poor. Paden (2011) argues that black civil rights groups' efforts to address policies to eliminate poverty have diminished since the 1960s. In general, such studies have echoed the complaints of activists, concluding that even groups that claim to exist on behalf of all blacks, and of women, usually fall short of full representation.

Even though black and Latino organizations claim to represent minority interests, then, their claims may not match their level of commitment to these issues (Alexander 2010; Cohen 1999; Strolovitch 2007). Studies show that many factors may limit civil rights organizations and minority legislators' responsiveness to minority interests, including their reliance on foundation and corporate funding and their close ties to the Democratic Party (Marquez 2003; Tate 2014).

To determine how well minority civil rights organizations represent the interests of black and Latino Americans, this chapter examines black and Latino public opinion data on economic and social issues from 1970 through 2016 in combination with lobbying disclosure reports, which I use to identify civil rights organizations' specific policy priorities. I find that major black and Latino civil rights organizations do effectively represent the interests of black and Latino communities. They spend time and resources lobbying on issues that are salient to minorities. They also lobby on policies that are controversial in minority communities in order to address the interests of disadvantaged subgroups within these communities.

I find, in addition, that reliance on corporate funding does not detract from the ability of civil rights organizations to be responsive to the evolving needs of the black and Latino communities. Indeed, the NAACP's agenda has expanded to cover as many progressive ideas in the 2000s as it did in the 1970s. Receiving monies from banks such as Wells Fargo, for example, has not stopped the NAACP or UnidosUS from devoting time to curbing aggressive efforts by banks to foreclose on minority homeowners. Nor do corporate contributions seem to limit civil rights groups' ability to press Congress to pass immigration reform—a position unpopular with many corporate donors.

While organizational networks such as Black Lives Matter and immigrant protest groups highlight the disparate treatment of blacks by law enforcement and Latinos by federal immigration enforcement officers, moreover, these networks do not possess the resources to provide sustained advocacy at the federal level. Major civil rights organizations, by contrast, do provide consistent advocacy before the federal government. The newer groups can either push mainstream groups to focus their attention on the issue, or they can provide leverage to traditional groups for bargaining with federal officials on issues they support.

Finally, I find that the CBC and CHC provide support for minority interests and for civil rights organizations despite the moderating influence of the Democratic Party. Minority legislators reflect the preferences of their minority constituents.

Organizational Maintenance and Capacity

How a group organizes, survives, and adapts to the changing political environment can play an important role in determining whether it can represent the interests of its constituent members (Walker 1991). Civil rights organizations are decentralized citizen groups whose membership and leaders include individuals from the general citizenry. Conversely, the vast majority of advocacy groups in Washington are professional and business associations (Schlozman, Verba, and Brady 2012). These groups have restricted memberships and are focused on representing the interests of professionals, such as lawyers, physicians, or businesses, and not necessarily on advocating for the broader interests of the general citizenry. Thus, citizen groups like the NAACP and LULAC might be expected to be more responsive to the general interests of minorities than, say, organizations designed to promote the professional interests of black and Latino engineers.

The membership of the NAACP and LULAC consists mainly of individuals from the general public, who can influence the policy and direction of the organization. These members are part of a network of chapters located across the nation that work with the national office to help set overall policy for the organizations nationally and locally. In 2020, the NAACP has more than two thousand chapters and more than five hundred thousand members; LULAC has one thousand councils located in the United States.[3] Additionally, the NAACP and LULAC have civil rights lobbying offices or bureaus in Washington, DC. The NAACP's Washington Bureau, led by Hilary Shelton, formulates the organization's legislative priorities. The bureau has a four-member team that works on policy issues in the areas of financial services, health care, and labor.[4] Staff members work on policy and attend meetings on Capitol Hill or at federal agencies.

The NAACP's legislative priorities are determined based on resolutions proposed by the members at the organization's annual convention. Resolutions must be adopted by the sixty-four-member board of directors before they become policy. The board instructs the Washington Bureau to develop legislation that addresses these issues, to support legislation that already exists, or to oppose legislation that threatens the stated position of the NAACP.[5] The Washington Bureau produces a list of legislative priorities for each congressional term. These legislative priorities are divided into seven major issue categories of civil rights and equal opportunity, criminal justice, labor, the economy, health, housing, and international issues. These major categories include specific support for legislation to eliminate or reduce sentencing disparities between crack and powder cocaine, to address predatory lending, to diminish financial disparities among schools, to address racial disparities in health care, and to lift U.S. trade and travel embargos against Cuba, among other priorities.

LULAC, similarly, has a sixty-member board that sets policy for the organization in consultation with local councils. The councils meet annually at LULAC's convention to set policy. LULAC uses resolutions and policy platforms to set the legislative agenda for the organization, which is implemented by the Washington office, under the leadership of Brent Wilkes since 1997.

Organizations such as UnidosUS (formerly the National Council of La Raza) and the NUL comprise a network of social providers who administer services to minority constituents. Unlike the members of NAACP and LULAC, the UnidosUS and NUL social providers do not play a formal role in setting the national policy direction of the organizations.

The National Urban League was established in 1910 to help integrate blacks moving from the agricultural-based South to the demands of living in an industry-based urban area (Weiss 1974). The organization has affiliates that provide social services such as job training and housing assistance to blacks in cities. These affiliates provide information to the leadership at the national headquarters that assists leadership in forming the organization's advocacy agenda. In 2019, the organization had more than ninety affiliates serving over three hundred communities nationwide.[6]

The NUL has a Washington bureau that is responsible for formulating its legislative advocacy agenda. To help formulate this policy agenda, the bureau holds its annual Legislative Policy Conference in Washington, DC. According to the NUL's website, this conference "is an opportunity for our Urban League affiliate presidents, board members, young professionals, and Guild members to meet with U.S. representatives and congressional staff for policy updates and discussion."[7] As of 2019, Clinton Odom served as the executive director of the bureau.

For UnidosUS, the local-level providers affiliate with the national office by paying a fee, which establishes the social provider as an affiliate of UnidosUS. The national staff spends much of its efforts on providing technical assistance and helping affiliates obtain government and private funding for their program operations. UnidosUS considered separating the affiliate network from its policy-making body and focusing instead on advocacy for Latino interests, broadly understood, but former organizational president Yzaguirre said that the link to social services providers was important for helping the national office formulate public policies that would meet the needs of Latinos.[8] UnidosUS has 272 affiliates located across the United States, as well national headquarters in Washington, DC.[9]

The UnidosUS executive director and twenty-four-member board of directors craft legislative priorities based on board directives.[10] Janet Murguia has led UnidosUS since 2005. UnidosUS has a team of lobbyists, with Eric

Rodriguez serving as the chief lobbyist. The structure of UnidosUS, as well as of the LULAC, is conducive to channeling the interests of minorities to organizational leaders.

Civil rights groups have also formed coalitions to help advance their broad interests. These coalitions consist of memberships of individuals and institutions. The LCCR, for instance, is a broad coalition of civil rights groups that includes organizations that advocate for the rights of women, blacks, Latinos, and gays and lesbians. The LCCR has a board of directors that is responsible for setting policy. It advocates only on issues that have broad support from its membership. The executive director of LCCR was Wade Henderson from 1996 through 2017.

Similarly, Latino groups have formed a coalition of nonprofit Latino organizations to advance their overlapping interests. The National Hispanic Leadership Agenda is a group of forty Latino national and regional organizations that work together to advance the interests of Latinos. The organization is a 501(c)(3) entity whose power comes from the coordination and ability of its constituent groups to formulate a collective Latino agenda. The NHLA has created voting scorecards to hold legislators accountable on policy important to the Latino community.

As this overview suggests, the organizational structure of the major civil rights organizations that advocate for minorities in Washington poses no significant barrier to adequate and responsive representation of minority interests. Rather, the major civil rights organizations for blacks and Latinos actively invite feedback from constituent members and advocates, as well as work to formulate policy priorities that respond directly to this feedback. If organizations do not have the resources or capacity to respond to minority concerns, however, then they might fail to effectively represent minority interests at the federal level. The next section examines this issue in greater detail.

Organizational Capacity

The infusion of money from corporations and foundations plays a significant role in expanding the organizational capacity of civil rights organizations. Table 3.1 shows the gross receipts and assets from 2015 for the largest tax-exempt organizations that are classified in the "Civil Rights, Social Action and Advocacy" category by the National Center for Charitable Statistics.[11] Among the 18,812 organizations in this category, the NAACP, UnidosUS, and the NAACP's Legal Defense Fund are the only three minority civil rights groups that rank in the top thirty in terms of gross receipts;

Table 3.1. Gross Receipts and Assets for Civil Rights and Social Action Organizations

Organizations	Gross Receipts	Assets
AARP	$34,151,686,394.00	$2,254,580,583.00
NRA	$368,019,026.00	$214,839,625.00
Legal Aid Society	$259,617,106.00	$78,084,797.00
ACLU Foundation and ACLU Inc.	$203,784,309.00	$429,640,775.00
Southern Poverty Law Center	$138,781,720.00	$353,174,928.00
Anti-Defamation League and Foundation	$95,901,489.00	$142,364,686.00
NAACP, LDF, Local Chapters	**$74,917,247.00**	**$72,031,026.00**
American Jewish Committee	$73,495,515.00	$152,719,181.00
Ipas	$71,465,395	$111,122,718.00
American Bar Association Fund for Justice and Education	$68,001,232.00	$23,786,433.00
Freedom Forum Newseum Inc.	$56,472,014.00	$50,270,557.00
Lambda Legal Defense and Education Fund Inc.	$54,719,793.00	$22,530,139.00
Christian Advocates Serving Evangelism Inc.	$53,339,038.00	$53,101,754.00
Alliance Defending Freedom	$51,537,691.00	$32,795,628.00
American Association of University Women	$47,388,716.00	$132,249,840.00
UnidosUS (National Council of La Raza)	**$45,653,692.00**	**$62,087,640.00**
Ability 360 Inc.	$43,322,556.00	$54,950,647.00
Californians to Protect Our Right to Vote	$42,503,407.00	$63,187.00
Human Rights Campaign Inc.	$39,202,307.00	$13,384,278.00
Fourth Freedom Inc.	$39,202,307.00	$17,835,566.00
PHRMA California Initiative Fund	$38,833,009.00	$38,407,429.00
Ms. Foundation for Women	$37,351,270.00	$40,746,775.00
New Israel Fund	$35,084,152.00	$22,445,634.00
Brooklyn Defender Services	$33,106,066.00	$6,459,156.00
Children's Defense Fund	$32,357,947.00	$27,749,303.00
Civic Ventures	$31,399,957.00	$14,375,876.00
Individual Advocacy Group Inc.	$29,261,395.00	$8,498,336.00
Institute for Justice	$28,758,447.00	$82,454,637.00
Center for Reproductive Rights	$27,469,194.00	$33,535,731.00
Disability Rights California	$23,751,649.00	$18,445,709.00
Mean	$1,209,879,468.00	
Median	$46,521,204.00	

Source: GuideStar.

non-minority-specific social action organizations such as the AARP and the National Rifle Association (NRA) have traditionally had vastly more resources. When the NAACP's national headquarters, local chapters, and the Legal Defense Fund are combined, they rank in the top ten in this broad category. When the list is restricted to organizations that address specifically minority-interest issues, then UnidosUS, the NAACP, and the Legal Defense Fund are the top organizations in gross receipts. The gross receipts of the National Urban League, which is not included by the National Center for Charitable Statistics in the "Civil Rights, Social Action and Advocacy" category, would, if included, appear to rank in the top fifteen at $55 million. LULAC is also not included in the category, but unlike the NUL, it would rank far outside the top fifteen by gross receipts, at $863,705.[12] Coalition organizations such as the NHLA and the LCCR are outside of the top fifty in gross receipts. In 2015, the NHLA had only $438,832 in gross receipts, and the LCCR brought in $2.9 million.

Minority civil rights organizations have attracted substantial revenue and accumulated assets partly as a result of their 501(c)(3) tax-exempt, or public charity, status designated by the federal government. Despite relatively flat growth in membership, these organizations have thrived due to receiving large contributions from corporations, foundations, and government grants. As a result, the headquarters of the national organizations have more resources today than they did at the height of the civil rights movement. In 2015, the NAACP's revenue, at $27.4 million, was more than three times its 1964 revenue of $8.7 million (in 2015 dollars).[13] In 2014, UnidosUS's revenue was $33.8 million, more than fifteen times its 1969 revenue of $2.68 million (in 2014 dollars).[14] In the 1960s and 1970s, before the NAACP was a 501(c)(3) organization, the group received most of its funding from its members; however, relying on membership to fund its advocacy efforts proved unsustainable. The group experienced financial troubles due to its inability to pay for its staff and organizational activities. Funding from outside groups such as corporations, private foundations, and the federal government stabilized the financial health of the organization and helped increase its lobbying capacity.

Lobbying Capacity

With the influx of corporate donations and grants from private foundations and the federal government, civil rights organizations have increased their lobbying capacity. These resources have allowed the organizations to increase their staff by hiring more in-house lobbyists. They also hire outside lobbying firms when needed, as the NAACP did when it brought in a professional firm to lobby on the 2008 economic stimulus bill. UnidosUS has always been a 501(c)(3) organization, and it received its initial funding from a Ford Foundation grant. It also relies on revenue received from affiliates. Tax-exempt status has permitted the group to expand its revenue, to rely less on foundation funding, and to increase its lobbying efforts.

According to the Washington Representatives database—compiled by Schlozman, Verba, and Brady (2012) in 2011—141 organizations represented African Americans, 135 represented Latinos, and 54 represented all minorities in Washington, DC, but none of these organizations can match the political power and lobbying strength of the NAACP, UnidosUS, or the LCCR.[15] Newer nonprofit advocacy groups such as the Black Youth Project, 100 NFP, and Presente Action are far behind the NAACP and UnidosUS in revenue and staff. In 2015, for example, the revenue of the Black Youth Project was $63,365, compared to the NAACP's $27.4 million. Presente Action had revenue of $114,884 that same year, compared to $33.8 million for UnidosUS in 2014. The smaller, more recently established groups, moreover, do not spend much time lobbying the federal government. These organizations do not report lobbying activity, which indicates that they would have spent less than $20,000 each year on lobbying.

Table 3.2 shows that from 2015 to 2016, the average lobbying expenditures of the top thirty grossing organizations in the Civil Rights and Social Action category was $1.1 million.[16] This average is driven largely by the presence of the AARP and NRA in the list, however. The AARP spent $16.2 million on lobbying over this period, and the NRA spent $6.7 million. The AARP ranked eighth among all groups in lobbying expenditures from 1998 to 2017 at $269 million. The NAACP, UnidosUS, and LCCR are among the top-spending minority groups that lobby the federal government.[17] Yet these groups are at or just below the overall Civil Rights and Social Action lobbying expenditures average of $1.1 million. The combined total of the NAACP and LDF is $1.1 million, and UnidosUS falls below the category average with lobbying expenditures of $514,000.[18]

Figure 3.1 shows that lobbying expenditures have increased for most of the major civil rights organizations since 1999. The LCCR and NAACP have steadily increased the amount of funds dedicated to lobbying. In 1999, the LCCR and NAACP spent only $250,539 and $57,625, respectively, on lobbying, compared to more than $1.3 million and $544,000 in 2016.[19] UnidosUS had an uptick in lobbying expenditures from 1999 through 2010, increasing from $288,124 to $583,438, with a drop-off after 2011 when the organization returned to its 1999 levels of spending. MALDEF and NUL have remained relatively flat in their level of spending.

Interestingly, the LCCR, which ranked outside of the top fifty in gross receipts in 2015, leads all minority civil rights groups in lobbying expenditures at $1.2 million, well above the average for the top-thirty groups by gross receipts. Even though the NAACP, LDF, and UnidosUS have higher gross receipts than the LCCR, the LCCR, as a 501(c)(4) organization, can engage in unlimited lobbying, whereas the NAACP and UnidosUS cannot because they are 501(c)(3)s. LULAC is also a 501(c)(4), yet the organiza-

Table 3.2. Lobbying Expenditures for Civil Rights and Social Action Organizations (2015–2016)

Organizations	Lobbying, 2015–2016
AARP	$16,269,000
NRA	$6,793,564
Legal Aid Society	$0
ACLU Foundation and ACLU Inc.	$2,752,460
Southern Poverty Law Center	$0
Anti-Defamation League and Foundation	$320,000
NAACP, LDF, Local Chapters	$1,070,153
American Jewish Committee	$260,000
Ipas	$0
American Bar Association Fund for Justice and Education	$2,017,500
Freedom Forum Newseum Inc.	$0
Lambda Legal Defense and Education Fund Inc.	$0
Christian Advocates Serving Evangelism Inc.	$0
Alliance Defending Freedom	$0
American Association of University Women	$346,000
UnidosUS (National Council of LaRaza)	$514,000
Ability 360 Inc.	$0
Californians to Protect Our Right to Vote	$0
Human Rights Campaign Inc.	$2,070,000
Fourth Freedom Inc.	$0
PHRMA California Initiative Fund	$0
Ms. Foundation for Women	$0
New Israel Fund	$0
Brooklyn Defender Services	$0
Children's Defense Fund	$0
Civic Ventures	$0
Individual Advocacy Group Inc.	$0
Institute for Justice	$30,000
Center for Reproductive Rights	$514,331
Disability Rights California	$0
Mean	$1,098,567
Median	$0

tion reported lobbying only twice from 1999 to 2016. In 2009, the group spent $10,000 on lobbying, followed by $20,000 in 2010.

The decision to incorporate as a 501(c)(3), or public charity, has increased the advocacy capacity of civil rights organizations, but it places them at a competitive disadvantage compared to other tax-exempt groups. Public charities are regulated by the "substantial test," whereby they cannot devote significant time and resources to explicitly political activity—such as urging legislators to vote for or against a bill (Berry and Arons 2003). As a general rule of thumb, the substantial test dictates that 501(c)(3)

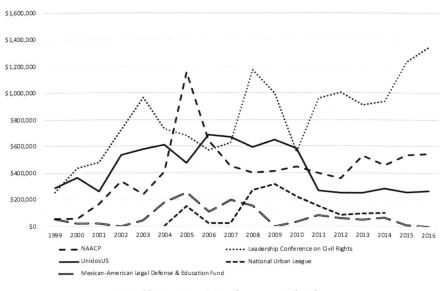

3.1. Lobbying Expenditures for Major Civil Rights
Organizations, 1999–2016 (in 2016 dollars)

organizations can spend no more than 20 percent of their revenue on lobbying activities. This rule is subject to broad interpretation by the IRS, and groups are reluctant to portray any advocacy work as lobbying—and in fact underreport the time and resources they devote to lobbying. Groups that choose 501(c)(4) status, by contrast, can perform unlimited lobbying, but any donations they receive are not tax-deductible contributions. Most organizations in the Civil Rights, Social Action, and Advocacy category are 501(c)(3) organizations, with some politically active nonprofits combining 501(c)(3) and 501(c)(4) entities, such as the ACLU and the Anti-Defamation League (Berry and Arons 2005). Public charity status is the only tax-exempt structure that places restrictions on lobbying. The 501(c)(4), or social welfare, groups and the 501(c)(6) groups, or business associations, can engage in lobbying without limit. Some of these groups can also form PACs and give money to political candidates. Many of the NAACP's local chapters are 501(c)(4)s, but these chapters do not engage in extensive lobbying at the federal level.

Minority civil rights organizations are well funded and devote significant resources to insider lobbying, but in comparison to the organizations that usually oppose them in the policy arena, such as business associations, and even to other groups in the "social welfare" category, such

Table 3.3. Lobby Expenditures Average by Type of Organization

Organizations	2011	2001
Business Associations	$739,000	$148,000
Corporations	$692,000	$102,000
Minorities	$158,000	$22,000
African Americans	$73,000	$10,000
Latinos	$57,000	$37,000

Source: Kay Lehman Schlozman, Traci Burch, Philip Edward Jones, Hye Young You, Sidney Verba, and Henry E. Brady, *Washington Representatives Study (Organized Interests in Washington Politics)—1981, 1991, 2001, 2006*, 2011 (2018), https://doi.org/10.7910/DVN/27317, Harvard Dataverse, V.1.

as the NRA, they spend less money on lobbying and are at a disadvantage. From 2010 to 2011, business associations on average spent $739,000 on lobbying, compared to only $158,000 for groups representing all minorities, $73,000 for groups representing black Americans, and $57,000 for groups representing Latinos. The highest-spending minority organization, the LCCR, at $1.5 million, spent more than the business association average, but its spending still ranked far below the top two major umbrella business-advocacy organizations, the U.S. Chamber of Commerce (at $169 million) and the Business Roundtable (at $2.8 million). The USCC has spent more money than any organization in lobbying the federal government; from 1998 to 2017, it spent $1.4 billion on lobbying.

Through lobbying, civil rights groups increase the scope and scale of black and Latino issues they can address that come before Congress. In the Democrat-controlled 110th Congress (2007–2008), under a Republican president, the NAACP, UnidosUS, and LCCR combined lobbied on 3 percent of the 11,081 bills introduced in the House and Senate. The NAACP, moreover, lobbies on more issues in the 2000s than it did in the 1970s.[20] The NAACP lobbied on 108 bills in the 110th Congress, or 0.98 percent of all bills, compared to 17 bills in 1978–1979, representing 0.12 percent of the 13,666 bills introduced in Congress.[21] From 1975 to 1979, the NAACP devoted most of its attention to the renewal of the Voting Rights Act and the passage of the Humphrey-Hawkins Full Employment Act. In the 111th Congress (2009–2010), when Democrats controlled Congress and the presidency, the NAACP's lobbying affected around 3 percent of bills. Although the NAACP has increased its lobbying efforts, its lobbying power still pales in comparison to that of the USCC. The USCC lobbies in almost every policy dimension, ranging from the economy to science and technology. In the 110th Congress, the USCC lobbied on 5.6 percent, or 622 bills, and in the following Congress it lobbied on 4.4 percent, or 470 bills. Figures 3.2 and 3.3 show the policy dimensions lobbied on by civil rights organizations in the 110th and 111th Congresses.

The largest and longest-established black and Latino rights organizations are in the best position, structurally and in terms of resource and lobbying capacity, to be responsive to minority interests. Their organizational structure encourages them to receive and respond to feedback from constituent members and affiliates, and their financial and organizational resources permit them to lobby consistently and actively in Congress in a way that more recently established, less well funded, and less democratically organized minority advocacy organizations cannot. Critics of the major black and Latino civil rights organizations have argued, however, that these organizations fail to respond to and represent minority interests adequately. Although civil rights groups have adapted to the financial uncertainty of relying only on membership dues to fund their activities, their reliance on outside funding to maintain operations creates concern about whether the organizations will effectively represent their members.

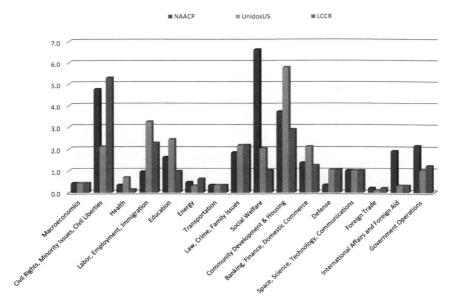

3.2. Percentage of Proposed Bills on Which Each Group Lobbied by Major Topic in 110th Congress (2007–2008)

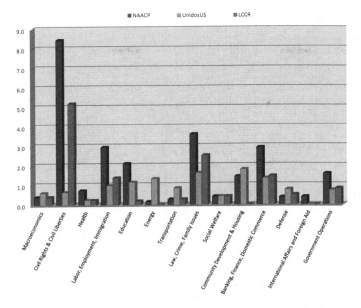

■ NAACP   ⊞ UnidosUS   ■ LCCR

3.3. Percentage of Proposed Bills on Which Each Group Lobbied
by Major Topic in 111th Congress (2009–2010)

The Challenge of Group Maintenance and Responsiveness

Corporate foundations associated with such businesses as AT&T, FedEx, and United Parcel Service, as well as private foundations such as the Ford Foundation and Robert Wood Johnson Foundation, contribute millions of dollars to civil rights groups like the NAACP and UnidosUS annually. Although these corporate and foundation contributions support the advocacy efforts of civil rights organizations, some scholars express concern that such major contributors might exercise undue influence over these efforts, compromising the groups' ability to actively and effectively advocate for the interests of minority constituents. Scholars have debated whether funding from outside groups such as foundations and corporations has influenced the degree of attention that groups devote to issues (Bartley 2007; Strach 2016). Concerned with maintaining their organizational existence, civil rights groups might become less radical or true to the goals of the insurgent movement they represent (Piven and Cloward 1977). In fact, civil rights groups are likely to have their ideas moderated or co-opted to meet the needs of funding organizations (Haines 1984; Marquez 2003).

Specifically, Marquez (2003) found that the dependency of Latino advocacy groups on funding from large foundations limited the organizations' ability to address Latino interests. Reliance on foundation funding can also shift the role of a group from political advocacy to one of social services provision (Minkoff 1999). Finally, corporate foundations usually spend most of their resources supporting candidates who tend to oppose many of the interests of blacks and Latinos. Thus, many scholars are skeptical that civil rights groups can take substantial donations from corporations without becoming ideologically indebted to them.

Despite claims that civil rights organizations have become less radical in their demands and advocacy efforts, few, if any, studies have examined systematically whether this proposition is true. Although the studies cited here raise normative concerns about mass-based groups relying on outside funds to maintain their activities, they do not show whether foundation funding impedes civil rights groups' advocacy for minority interests in federal policy making. In the social movement literature, some scholars have found that in the 1950s and 1960s, accepting outside money had limited effects on the protest activities and policy objectives of civil rights organizations (McAdam 1982; Morris 1984). These studies do not tell us, however, whether civil rights groups' increasing reliance on outside funding to maintain their organizational activities has an impact on the contemporary advocacy efforts of these organizations.

To assess whether civil rights organizations have become less responsive to minority interests and radical in their demands as they rely more on corporate and private foundation funding, I examine to what degree the stated advocacy agendas of minority civil rights organizations match the policy preferences of blacks and Latinos, as measured with survey data. If groups are active on issues that blacks and Latinos rank as high priorities in opinion polls, then this is one indicator that reliance on outside funding does not hinder or divert their attention from the interests of marginalized groups. Assessing policy congruence between constituent opinion and the actions of legislators is used in political representation studies to determine whether legislators are effectively representing their constituents' interests (Bartels 2008; Miller and Stokes 1963; Tate 2010). I apply this method to advocacy group behavior. Second, I qualitatively examine the agendas of civil rights organization to identify how frequently they pay attention to issues that are important to racial or ethnic minorities but might divide the Democratic coalition—issues such as immigration reform, reparations, and racial profiling.

Responsiveness to Black Interests

Black Americans advocate for strong federal government intervention to eliminate racial disparities in employment, education, and housing (Dawson 2001). Thus, support for liberal social welfare policies and race-specific policies have consistently been part of the black American policy agenda. However, Tate (2010) argues that with the incorporation of minorities into the political system, political leaders began to play a role in moderating black mass public opinion.

Although polling does show that black public opinion has become more moderate on certain issues, such as aid from government and spending on social welfare, much polling also indicates that blacks consider social welfare a top national issue. American National Election Studies (ANES) data show the policy preferences of black Americans have remained consistent since the 1960s: African Americans list social welfare, the economy, unemployment, and race relations as the most important problems facing the country.[22] Figures 3.4 and 3.5 show how black Americans' preferences have changed in level of support for these social welfare and race relations issues over time. Social welfare issues have been a major concern for all groups from the 1960s to the 2000s; however, black Americans and Latinos

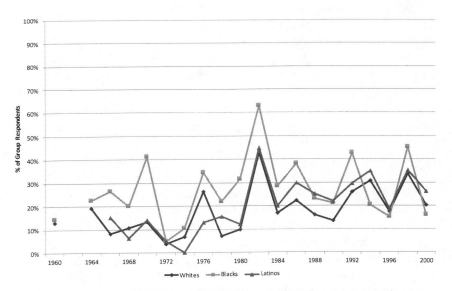

3.4. Most Important Problem by Race/Ethnicity: Social Welfare (1960–2000)

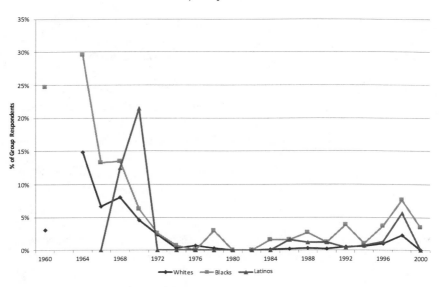

3.5. Most Important Problem by Race/Ethnicity: Racial Problems (1960–2000)

rate them as a more important problem than do whites. Not surprisingly, blacks and Latinos considered race relations the most important problem in the 1960s, but this level of concern has since declined in salience for all groups—although Gallup shows that racial relations measure as a stronger interest for blacks than does the ANES data.[23]

Despite claims to the contrary, there is significant evidence to indicate that major black civil rights organizations have responded well to minority interests. A June 2016 Pew Research poll showed that 77 percent of blacks agreed that the NAACP had been somewhat effective in helping blacks achieve equality in the country, while 66 percent expressed the same sentiment for the NUL.[24] In addition to this subjective evaluation from black citizens, I find that from 2007 through 2010 (the 110th and 111th Congresses), the NAACP devoted significant effort to lobbying Congress on behalf of minorities. In the 110th Congress (2007–2008), the top five issue areas lobbied on by the NAACP were social welfare (6.6 percent), civil rights (4.8 percent), community development and housing (3.7 percent), government operations, and international affairs and foreign aid (1.8 percent; see figure 3.2). Although the NAACP's rate of lobbying was highest on social welfare issues, the NAACP lobbied on the largest number of bills in the "government operations" category. An analysis of the data shows that 18 percent of the NAACP's policy agenda fell in this category because there are more bills introduced in government operations than in social welfare—977 bills in the Congress under consideration compared to 196 in social welfare. Social welfare was second on the NAACP's policy agenda, followed by law, crime, and family issues; banking and finance; and education.

In the 111th Congress (2009–2010), the NAACP's focus on social welfare declined significantly from the prior Congress. Instead, its top areas of lobbying included civil rights (8.4 percent); law, crime, and family (3.6 percent); and labor and employment and immigration (3 percent). The NAACP has always had a dual agenda that focuses on civil rights and social welfare. When Democrats controlled the Congress and presidency in the 111th Congress, civil rights groups took the opportunity to push legislation in an area of primary focus. The NAACP is also responsive to labor needs as they relate to civil rights. The organization focuses on antidiscrimination suits, supports living wages for all workers, and backs protections for unionization and against employment discrimination in the private and public sectors.

Tate (2014) argues that in the 2010s, black legislators were less likely to support "radical" proposals, such as guaranteed jobs legislation, than they were when they supported legislation like the Humphrey-Hawkins guaranteed jobs bills in the 1970s. Black legislators and their constituents do continue to support "radical" economic proposals, however. Additionally, blacks strongly support increased government spending for social welfare programs, and they overwhelmingly support reparations for African Americans. From the 109th Congress (2005–2006) to the 116th Congress (2019–2020), the NAACP listed reparations in its legislative priorities document and lobbied on the reparations bill introduced by a member of the Congressional Black Caucus. Rep. Shelia Jackson Lee (D-TX) introduced the most recent version of the reparations bill in the 116th Congress. The reparations bill was first introduced in the 101st Congress (1989–1990) by Rep. John Conyers (D-MI), who introduced it every congressional session until he resigned from Congress in 2017. In 2007, the NAACP and CBC supported legislation by Rep. Conyers and Sen. Russ Feingold (D-WI) to end racial profiling by law enforcement officials. The NAACP lists the anti–racial profiling bill as one of its top legislative priorities and lobbies for the passage of the bill in each congressional session. In 2012, the Senate held hearings on the bill after the shooting of a black teenager, Trayvon Martin, by George Zimmerman, a self-proclaimed Latino neighborhood-watch person. The NAACP focused on eliminating racial profiling well before the shootings of Michael Brown and Tamir Rice and before the emergence of the Black Lives Matter movement.

Harris-Perry and other critics argue that the NAACP is becoming increasingly irrelevant, however, because the group does not pay sufficient attention to black gay and lesbian issues. Although this is a legitimate concern for those who want black civil rights organizations to represent the interests of all blacks, and not just some, public opinion polls show that the majority of blacks do not consider LGBTQ issues among the most important problems facing the country, and the majority of blacks also oppose gay marriage. As Cohen demonstrates, the failure of black organizations to address issues that relate to the black LGBT community can have devastating consequences for all blacks—and perhaps this an argument that civil rights organizations have come to appreciate, as they do devote some efforts to gay and lesbian issues, despite the fact that these issues lack broad support from black Americans. Although these efforts represent a small proportion of their overall advocacy agenda, they should not be dismissed completely.

Moreover, these minority-group-supported issues have become part of the Democratic agenda. During the 110th Congress (2007–2008) and 111th Congress (2009–2010), the NAACP and its LDF supported the passage of the Matthew Shepard and James Byrd Hate Crime Act, which enacted tougher federal penalties against crimes based on race, ethnicity, and sexual orientation. Additionally, the NAACP lobbied on a bill sponsored by Rep. Barney Frank (D-MA) to prohibit employment discrimination on the basis of sexual orientation or gender identity. Such bills are not necessarily priorities for Democrats, but the party pays more attention to these issues that it did in the past. In the 105th Congress (1997–1998), Rep. Charles Schumer (D-NY) introduced hate-crimes legislation. In the 111th Congress, a hate-crimes bill was passed by Congress and signed into law by President Obama.

Although Michelle Alexander has argued that the NAACP and the LCCR did not advocate forcefully enough for legislation to reduce sentencing disparities between crack and powder cocaine, the lobbying evidence indicates otherwise. The passage of these bills was the result of longtime advocacy by a coalition of groups including the NAACP, the LCCR, and minority and women legislators. It is not just the passage of law that is significant but also the amount of attention devoted by Congress to these issues. Influenced by civil rights organizations' advocacy, the number of hearings that these bills received increased. Prominent leaders testified at committee hearings and submitted written comments to be included in the congressional record. Wade Henderson, director of the LCCR, testified at several hearings and worked with the staff of legislators responsible for crafting the Fair Sentencing Act.

Of the smaller-revenue nonprofit groups that represent blacks, none has reported lobbying the federal branch. Although these groups engage in grassroots activity, they do not participate in much insider lobbying activity with congressional representatives. The Black Youth Project and other small-revenue organizations have little to no presence at the federal level. Black Lives Matter has captured significant attention in the news media, but its efforts have not led to federal legislation, primarily because the GOP, which controls Congress, has opposed the group's efforts. These groups have been instrumental, however, in getting major civil rights organizations and politicians to pressure the police to wear body cameras and to increase funding for police training.

Responsiveness to Latino Interests

Despite the diversity contained within the Latino community, Latinos have faced a history of discrimination in employment, housing, and education (Garcia Bedolla 2009; Hero 1992). As do blacks and other marginalized groups, Latinos favor strong government intervention to address these disparities (Hero 1992). Although Marquez (2003) argues that groups such as UnidosUS and MALDEF may not be as responsive to Latino interests because of their reliance on corporate and government funding, the evidence does not support this concern.

On most public-opinion polls, Latinos list immigration reform, education, the economy, and unemployment or jobs as the most important issues facing the Latino community or the country. In the 2006 Latino National Survey, respondents identified the most important problem facing the Latino community as illegal immigration (29.5 percent), unemployment or jobs (12.1 percent), education or public schools (9.9 percent), the economy (6.7 percent), and race relations (4.6 percent) (figures 3.6).[25] The Pew Research Center conducted a similar survey from 2004 to 2013 wherein interviewers asked respondents to rate the issues that were extremely important to them personally. The survey found that in 2013, Latinos identified education (55 percent), jobs and the economy (54 percent), health care (50 percent), and immigration (34 percent) as the most important problems.[26] Latino support for immigration reform has increased over time. Even though the issue does not pertain to Puerto Ricans, they too have supported it. This was the case in the 1970s as well as 2007–2010.

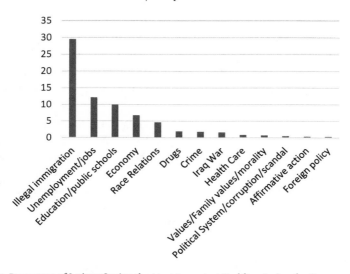

3.6. Percentage of Latinos Stating the Most Important Problem Facing the Community
Source: Luis R. Fraga, John A. Garcia, Rodney Hero, Michael Jones-Correa, Valerie Martinez-Ebers, and Gary M. Segura, *Latino National Survey (LNS), 2006* (ICPSR20862-v6), Inter-University Consortium for Political and Social Research [distributor], University of Michigan, June 5, 2013, http://doi .org/10.3886/ICPSR20862.v6.

The major Latino advocacy groups devote significant time and resources to advocating for the issues identified by Latinos as their top priorities. UnidosUS played a key role in working with Senator Kennedy and LULAC to craft a bipartisan solution to the immigration problem. UnidosUS identified immigration reform as its top policy priority and spent significant time addressing it at the federal level. From 2006 to 2008, UnidosUS spent the most time lobbying in the labor and immigration policy area, which the organization considers a critical economic issue. According to a UnidosUS representative, "We understand that if one cannot establish legal status, then it is difficult to obtain protections that are required to acquire employment and command protections against employers taking advantage of their employees."[27] Even though most Latinos are citizens, many have family members who are affected by immigration policies. The NHLA produces a policy agenda report in which immigration reform is listed as its top policy issue.

The UnidosUS agenda similarly reflects the goals and policy preferences of Latinos. Figures 3.2 and 3.3 showed that from 2007 to 2010, UnidosUS spent most of its lobbying efforts on labor, employment, and immigration issues, followed by banking, education, community development and housing, and law and crime. Thus, the top three issues identified by Latinos in surveys are the focus of UnidosUS's advocacy agenda. The Latino community's focus on immigration is not just an issue that is driven by mass public opinion; public opinion is also shaped by the advocacy efforts of Latino civil rights organizations and Latino legislators (Barreto and Segura 2014).

UnidosUS is more than an advocacy group. As we have seen, it also supports affiliates that provide services directly to the Latino community, from health care to housing counseling. UnidosUS spends time trying to ensure government funding for its constituents and specific affiliates. UnidosUS has also been able to secure funding from corporate sources, such as Verizon.

Even though Latino organizations agree that immigration is a top priority, they take different positions regarding which legislative or executive solutions are best to solve the problem. The smaller groups, such as Presente Action, support amnesty for all undocumented immigrants, but UnidosUS does not fully support this proposal (Martinez 2009). All Latino civil rights groups do agree, however, that the present immigration system does not address the needs of Latinos. Latino civil rights groups continue to push the Democratic Party and the Republican Party to make immigration a top priority of Congress. Latino groups also agree that shortcomings in education should be addressed, with the smaller groups pushing for vouchers for charter schools while the larger-revenue, more traditional organizations advocate for more funding for existing public schools (Martinez 2009).

Organizational structure and capacity create a strong foundation for larger civil rights organizations to advocate in Washington in a way that smaller, more diffuse, less well-funded groups cannot. Conversely, that same structure and capacity (which includes staff and Washington bureaus, with associated costs, as well as the cost of lobbying to protect the organization and its funding), limit these organizations in their ability to respond to rapidly changing concerns or to concerns that have managed to reach only portions of their constituent population, such as younger members or more "woke" segments of the membership. In other words, there are trade-offs between size and capacity on the one hand and responsiveness on the other. But even when these trade-offs are taken into account, the largest, most established minority rights organizations do an admirable job of advocating on issues identified as important to the majority of their members, as well as advocating on some issues that are important only to subgroups—and they take instruction in a responsive and organized manner regarding what to advocate for from constituent members and affiliates, which keeps them flexible and responsive, ensuring that their identified policy priorities are a strong match to the priorities of the minorities they represent.

Corporate and Private Foundation Influence
and Civil Rights Groups

Even though civil rights organizations receive most of their donations from corporations, private foundations, and government sources, these contributions do not diminish the scope or intensity of civil rights groups' advocacy for minority interests. As demonstrated in figures 3.2 and 3.3, which investigate civil rights organizations' responsiveness to African American and Latino interests, these organizations devote most of their efforts to civil rights, social welfare, and immigration, issues that blacks and Latinos consider the most important problems facing the country or community. There is no clear indication that the acceptance of large donations from AT&T, Walmart, and the Ford Foundation by the NAACP, for instance, has influenced the group to lobby more on telecommunications issues or other issues of interest to those corporations.

Of course, it is possible that donor relationships might have suppressed the NAACP's lobbying efforts on these issues, but there is no clear pattern to show that it has. My examination of legislative priorities and lobbying disclosure reports reveal no telecom or retail-related activity. The NAACP had a pending lawsuit claiming that Wells Fargo engaged in discriminatory lending practices against minority communities. In 2012, the U.S. Department of Justice filed a predatory lending lawsuit against Wells Fargo. Both parties settled, with the bank agreeing to pay a record $184 million in damages to black and Latino borrowers.[28] The NAACP dropped its suit against Wells Fargo. The NAACP's annual report showed that Wells Fargo donated $1 million to the NAACP. Whether this was part of a broader settlement is unclear, but it does seem apparent that being in receipt of these funds from Wells Fargo did not influence the NAACP to support policies that Wells Fargo might favor.

These findings are not too surprising, considering that it is difficult to determine whether contributors use donations in an attempt to influence group behavior. Contributors usually give money for a variety of reasons, one of which is that the organization's program fits the goals and objectives of the funders—as is usually the case with corporate and private foundations and governmental agencies. Funders might want to be seen as good public citizens by making high-profile donations to groups that exhibit their commitment to the donor's cause. That is, corporate donors are most likely attempting not to influence civil rights organizations like the NAACP with their donations, but rather to associate themselves with those organizations and their missions in a positive way. Their donations do not come with significant strings attached; civil rights groups, in turn, understand this and make no attempt to alter their missions or policy agendas to bring them into line with donor priorities.

Corporate and other funding has increased the capacity of civil rights organizations without limiting their responsiveness to minority interests; however, minority civil rights organizations still have significantly fewer resources than businesses and other organizations in the civil rights and social advocacy arena.

Conclusion

The NAACP, NUL, UnidosUS, and the LCCR are the best-funded and best-staffed minority organizations to lobby the federal government consistently over time. They are in a position of advantage relative to their civil rights peers, but one of disadvantage compared to business associations, which have much deeper pockets when it comes to lobbying and vastly outnumber civil rights organizations. Civil rights organizations have greater resources and spend more money lobbying Congress today than they did in the 1970s. Lobbying disclosure reports most likely understate the level of advocacy these groups engage in on the Hill and the ability of these organizations to influence legislators. Groups are cautious about spending too much time or money on lobbying for fear of IRS sanctions, and they rely on insider lobbying tactics to pursue their legislative agenda. These tactics require resources to fund hiring outside lobbying firms and salaried inside lobbying personnel. As a result, many civil rights organizations rely on contributions from corporations and foundations to fund their operations. Although some have raised concerns that reliance on this funding will limit the ability of civil rights groups to effectively represent minority interests, the infusion of corporate donations has not shifted the focus of civil rights groups from their core mission of being forceful advocates for civil rights and economic justice. These groups not only lobby effectively on issues specific to blacks and Latinos but also have expanded their focus to lobby directly on gay and lesbian rights and women's issues. The NAACP has received much criticism for not being active on police brutality and shootings, but the group worked closely with Rep. Sheila Jackson (D-TX) and Sen. Ben Cardin (D-MD) to get racial profiling bills passed by Congress. Its lobbying agenda, moreover, reflects the preferences of its minority constituents.

The primary caveat to this analysis is that civil rights organizations, like most groups, are driven to maintain the survival of their organizations. For this reason, they spend a lot of time lobbying Congress to obtain money to fund their organizations and many of their programs. Most of the lobbying efforts of civil rights organizations are directed to the federal budget and appropriations. This lobbying does not seem to correlate to jobs programs or affordable housing.

This chapter shows what issues civil rights groups have focused on over time and areas where groups have expanded or contracted their focus. In recent years, Congress has paid more attention to civil rights. Civil rights groups played an important role in this shift. The priority of civil rights issues in the legislative agenda has increased significantly, although it continues to lag behind government operations, defense, and banking. Many surveys indicate that blacks and Latinos usually prioritize the economy and health care above all other issues. Although the main function of civil rights groups is to address civil rights issues, blacks and Latinos expect civil rights organizations to play an important role in supporting measures that reduce unemployment and bring jobs to their communities. Civil rights organizations do a good job of representing the interests of their members. They have also have expanded their focus to areas that are still fairly controversial in minority communities, such as support for LGBT rights and attention to eliminating HIV/AIDS. The LCCR, with its much larger membership, focuses on these issues too, even though it represents a much broader coalition of groups, which makes obtaining agreement among them more difficult.

The issues that come before Congress have expanded in scope over time, and civil rights groups have adjusted their attention accordingly while keeping their specific focus on civil rights. Consistent NAACP policy priorities include fairness for minorities in the criminal justice system and the enforcement of civil rights laws in employment and housing. Meanwhile, they have extended their focus to macroeconomic issues, including banking and finance.

Civil rights groups do not service constituencies that have the resources to bankroll their operations. Possession of 501(c)(3) status allows these groups to accept donations to subsidize their advocacy. The federal government subsidizes the advocacy efforts of civil rights organizations by granting them tax-exempt status—just as it does for a range of other organizations, from the National Football League to hospitals to unions. Despite accounts decrying the ineffectiveness of minority civil rights groups, these groups are the clear leaders in representing black and Latino interests at the federal level.

The next two chapters examine whether the strategy used by minority civil rights organizations to increase the number of black and Latino legislators led to the creation of a group of advocates in Congress who are responsive to minority interests.

FOUR

Diversity and Legislative Success in Committees

In 2007, Democrats gained control of both the House and the Senate after almost a decade of Republican rule.[1] The economic recession provided an opportunity for civil rights organizations and Democrats to direct attention to issues that disproportionately affected minority communities. Civil rights groups wanted to ensure that minority interests were included in the discussion and solutions proposed for how to solve the housing and financial crisis. House Speaker Nancy Pelosi (D-CA) and Senate Majority Leader Harry Reid (D-NV) acted quickly on their party's campaign promise to introduce progressive legislation designed to address the economic concerns of middle-class and low-income families. They proposed bills to increase the federal minimum wage and to reduce pay disparities between men and women. Democrats promised to pass legislation within the first hundred hours of the new congressional session. Most of the bills failed to become law, however, because President George W. Bush either threatened to veto or did veto the legislation.

Divided government hindered the ability of Democrats to enact their liberal policies. The circumstances changed when Democrats obtained complete control of government with the election of Sen. Barack Obama (D-IL) to the U.S. presidency. Although Democrats fell short of their ambitious goals, the various legislative proposals forwarded by the party foreshadowed the future liberal-leaning policy direction of House Democrats. For the first time since 1993, Democrats had the ability to set the national agenda and the power to pass legislation.

Civil rights organizations, whose policy interests are usually aligned with those of Democrats, also saw an opportunity to advance their policy initiatives. Although the economic recession and health-care reform dominated the congressional agenda in this period, civil rights organizations relished the opportunity to gain traction on issues they had long championed with the support of their congressional advocates. Since the early 2000s, the NAACP and the CBC had wanted the federal government to crack down on predatory lending and provide affordable housing options to minorities. As policy makers and the general public tried to make sense of the high rates of home foreclosures, the CBC and NAACP warned of the devastating impact that predatory lending practices had on minority communities beginning in 2001. Blacks and Latinos represented a disproportionate share of the housing foreclosures in the nation. CBC and CHC members represented these constituents and argued that eliminating predatory lending would be key in solving the housing crisis. CBC members pressed for greater regulation of financial institutions that charged high rates to people of color. The bills imposing these regulations were all listed as legislative priorities of the NAACP and lobbied on by the organization.

From 2001 through 2006, CBC members and Democrats introduced a number of anti–predatory lending bills. In 2001, Rep. Maxine Waters (D-CA) introduced a bill to prohibit mortgage lenders from engaging in deceptive lending practices and from steering consumers into the subprime market. One year later, Rep. Stephanie Tubbs Jones (D-OH) introduced a bill to prohibit subprime lenders from engaging in mortgage lending unless lending employees received training from the U.S. Department of Housing and Urban Development. Both bills were referred to House Financial Services, the committee responsible for overseeing housing and financial issues. Even though House Financial Services membership was racially and ethnically diverse, the bills did not receive a hearing or markup. The Republican Party was in control of the House during this time. The Senate held two hearings on the topic in the Democratic-controlled Senate from 2001 to 2002. The CBC Housing Task Force held district-level forums and national town-hall meetings to address predatory lending.[2] Meanwhile, UnidosUS and the CHC wanted the federal government to pass comprehensive immigration reform in an effort to ensure a clear path to citizenship for undocumented residents and their children—to no avail. Despite President George W. Bush's garnering of a sizable proportion of the Latino vote in his 2000 and 2004 election, the president and Congress failed to enact immigration reform.

Although the NAACP, UnidosUS, and the LCCR were optimistic about the chance to get their policy priorities written into law, they knew that unified Democratic control of government did not necessarily guarantee the passage of progressive civil rights legislation.[3] Even though Democrats had controlled all the elected branches of federal government from the 1930s to the 1950s, party leaders of that era refrained from addressing civil rights for fear of losing conservative Southern Democratic voters and legislators (Valelly 2004; Walton and Smith 2000). Even in the post–civil rights movement era, party leaders were hesitant to address policies aimed at eliminating racial and economic disparities in employment, housing, and health. In the early 1990s, former governor Bill Clinton (D-AR) campaigned for the U.S. presidency as a "New Democrat"—a Democrat who would not be beholden to the liberal interests of the party, such as organized labor and civil rights organizations. Clinton used this stance to distance the party from traditional civil rights issues supported by Democrats and liberal groups, such as affirmative action and liberal funding for social welfare policies, in order to increase his chance of winning the presidency and reelection (Frymer 1999; Smith 1996). During the first two years of his first term (1993–1994), Clinton was not as proactive on the civil rights front as some civil rights organizations and minority legislators would have preferred (Smith 1996). When Democrats lost control of the Congress to Republicans in 1994, Clinton signed GOP-sponsored legislation that imposed punitive restrictions on welfare for poor people and tougher mandatory sentencing for crime. He signed this legislation over the objections of minority civil rights organizations and liberal Democratic legislators.

Civil rights organizations believed that President Obama and a Democratic Congress would be more supportive of their agenda than had the Democratic Congress of the Clinton era. First, Obama had one of the most liberal voting records on civil rights in the U.S. Senate. In the 110th Congress (2007–2008), he scored a perfect 100 out of 100 on the NAACP voting scorecard and 96 out of 100 on the LCCR voting scorecard.[4] He was also a member of the liberal-leaning Congressional Black Caucus. Obama did not campaign as a New Democrat or a candidate embracing moderate to conservative policies, as Bill Clinton had, but rather openly embraced many policies espoused by liberal groups in the Democratic coalition, including taking a stance against the wars in Iraq and Afghanistan. Second, the Democratic majority was more liberal and diverse than the Democratic majorities of the 1930s to early 1990s had been. In 2007, Rep. Nancy Pelosi became the first woman elected to serve as Speaker of the House of Representatives. Pelosi was more liberal than the previous Democratic speaker, Rep. Tom Foley (D-WA). Rep. James Clyburn (D-SC), a member of the CBC, was elected to serve as the Democratic House Majority Whip. Committees were also structured to include more racial and ethnic diversity. Blacks and Latinos held subcommittee and full committee leadership posts on important committees that addressed civil rights and issues important to minorities.

This chapter examines the extent to which such committee diversity was important to the legislative success of minority civil rights organizations. That is, did civil rights organizations achieve greater legislative success in the diverse environment of the 110th and 111th Congresses? Were they more successful under unified Democratic control of the Congress and presidency? I begin with an overview of the level of diversity on House committees in the period following the civil rights movement. I then consider specifically whether the inclusion of more black and Latino legislators on committees led to greater attention for legislation supported by minority civil rights organizations. Specifically, I examine in this chapter how far bills supported by minority civil rights groups advanced in Congress under Democratic Party control of the House under Speaker Pelosi (2007–2010) through analysis of markup hearings, paying attention also to the effects of partisan control of the presidency.[5] The chapter that follows continues this investigation through analysis of committee testimony. Taken together, both chapters provide a measure at civil rights organizations' influence in Congress through their alliance with minority legislative advocates.

Diversity in the Committee System after the Civil Rights Movement

As we saw in chapter 2, before the civil rights movement of the 1950s and 1960s, civil rights organizations had limited success in getting Congress to address civil rights issues. Although these groups had civil rights champions such as Rep. Adam Clayton Powell Jr. (D-NY) and Rep. Emanuel Celler (D-NY), conservative Southern Democrats strongly opposed civil rights advancement (Hamilton 1991; Schickler 2016; Zelizer 2004). White Southern Democrats dominated the committee membership and leadership positions and used their power to set the agenda, ensuring that civil rights bills did not receive hearings or markups and never passed out of committee. In the House, Rep. Howard Smith (D-VA), chair of the Rules Committee, opposed any action on civil rights. In 1957, Southern Democrats also comprised 33 percent of the twelve members of the Rules Committee, which is responsible for determining whether bills make it to the House floor for a vote. In the 85th Congress (1957–1958), white Southerners held 55 percent of twenty committee leadership posts. Although Celler chaired the House Judiciary Committee, Southern white Democrats comprised 22 percent of the committee's membership. These Democrats represented constituencies that supported segregation and maintained white supremacy. There was no moderating electoral effect on white legislators, because blacks had little to no voting power. As a result, white Southerners gained seniority, which allowed them to ascend to committee chairmanships.

In the U.S. Senate, Southern Democrats used the filibuster to defeat the Civil Rights Act of 1957. The longtime segregationist Sen. Strom Thurmond (D-SC) holds the record for the longest filibuster in Senate history, having spent twenty-four hours and eighteen minutes filibustering the bill. From 1900 through the 1960s, the NAACP and LCCR tried to get Congress to change procedural mechanisms, including the filibuster in the Senate, in order to diminish the power of committee chairs in both chambers (Zelizer 2004). Several congressional reforms succeeded in reducing the power of committee chairs and returning power to party leaders. These changes weakened Southern Democrats and strengthened party leaders supportive of civil rights legislation for blacks. In response to civil rights protests, Congress passed the Voting Rights Act (1965), which protected the franchise of black citizens by outlawing barriers to voting. As a result of the Democratic Party's support for civil rights, as well as the efforts of GOP U.S. presidential candidates such as Barry Goldwater and Richard Nixon to distance the party from civil rights, many Southern white Democrats switched to the Republican Party. These measures made the Democratic Party more ideologically liberal and more receptive to civil rights legislation.

Thus, the decline of conservative Democrats led to a rise in power for minority legislators. Although Democrats overall became more receptive to black interests, black and Latino legislators understood that limiting their advocacy efforts to supporting the platform of the Democratic Party would not be sufficient to address the issues of their minority constituents. Minority legislators began to construct a diversity infrastructure to gather information and coordinate on issues important to blacks and Latinos (Minta and Sinclair-Chapman 2013). Black and Latino legislators formed the Congressional Black Caucus and Congressional Hispanic Caucus in the 1970s to promote the collective interests of minorities nationwide, not just blacks and Latinos who lived in their districts (Barnett 1982; Casellas 2010; Clay 1993; Henry 1977). In 2005, minority legislators formed a separate caucus, the Congressional Tri-Caucus, in response to governmental failures following Hurricane Katrina, with the aim of facilitating agenda coordination across minority groups. Caucuses allow for the sharing of resources across legislative offices, enhance communication and information sharing, and provide for the coordination of agendas and messages (Minta and Sinclair-Chapman 2013; Tyson 2016).

As minority legislators have increased in number and organized into sizable voting blocs, their ability to influence the congressional agenda has grown (Canon 1999). Minority legislators expanded information task forces within the caucuses to develop positions on a variety of issues, including the economy, social welfare, and civil rights (Barnett 1982; Bositis 1994). The CBC Foundation, for example, sponsors a legislative weekend to receive input on policy formation via task forces; members then use the information gained from the task forces to assist in advocacy for minority interests in House committees that have jurisdiction over civil rights, social welfare, health, and education.

Congress and interest groups draw attention to important issues using committee tools such as hearings and markups. Receiving committee action is usually the initial step a bill must clear to advance in the legislative process before it can become a law (Krutz 2005). Even if a bill does not become a law, committee hearings and markups give interest groups and their legislative advocates an opportunity to provide information to Congress about the groups' policy concerns, either through witness testimony at hearings or participation by legislative allies in committee markups on bills. The Senate, because of its low capacity, has not developed a diversity infrastructure comparable to that of the House (Minta and Sinclair-Chapman 2013). Thus, the Senate's ability to bring attention to minority interests is weak relative to that of the House.

Over time, the number of racial and ethnic minority committee chairs and leaders has grown in the House and, albeit at a slower rate, in the Senate. Minority legislators can marshal the power of committees to influence not only legislation but also federal agencies that enforce existing federal civil rights laws and other regulations salient to minorities (Minta 2009, 2011; Walton 1988). The change is reflected in the growing diversity evident in the committee system. Committee leadership and majority party leadership decide whether a bill should move out of committee. The infusion of minority legislators on congressional committees ensures that committees have more legislators who share the same commitment as civil rights organizations to advancing policy that benefits minorities. In the 95th Congress (1977–1978), blacks and Latinos comprised only 6.5 percent of Democratic Party membership and were not part of the party leadership;[6] by 2010, however, minorities accounted for an important part of the membership and leadership, with blacks and Latinos representing 20.8 percent of Democratic Party membership and 25 percent of party leaders in the 111th Congress.

Additionally, committee chairs became more racially and ethnically diverse. Full committee chairmanships had become more diverse in the 1970s than previously, but they still had not advanced beyond token representation. In the 95th Congress, blacks held only 8 percent of the committee chairs, and Latinos held no leadership positions. In the 111th Congress, in contrast, blacks held 15 percent and Latinos 5 percent of committee chairs. The most significant gains occurred at the subcommittee level, where blacks held 17.6 percent of subcommittee chairs and Latinos, 9.8 percent. The Senate meanwhile remained relatively unchanged, with blacks and Latinos representing an average of 3 percent of Senate membership in the 95th and the 111th Congresses.

Not only did the House become more diverse, but minority members were assigned to committees with jurisdiction over civil rights and other issues of importance to civil rights organizations. This was not by chance. Legislators request committees that best serve the interests of their constituents and enhance their reelection chances (Shepsle 1978). Consequently, minority legislators seek to serve on a variety of committees that provide specific benefits to their constituents, as well as to obtain information that will help them craft policy (Weingast and Marshall 1988; Krehbiel 1991). Thus, it is not surprising that the House Judiciary Committee, with its jurisdiction over civil rights and minority interest issues, is the second most racially and ethnically diverse committee in the House (figure 4.1). House Judiciary has not always been diverse. In the 95th Congress (1977–1978), blacks made up only 8 percent of the committee, which included no Latinos or Asian Americans. In the 110th Congress (2007–2008), blacks represented 20 percent and Latinos represented 5 percent of the membership, with no Asian American presence. When Democrats controlled the House from 2007 to 2010, Rep. John Conyers (D-MI) was chair of House Judiciary. Conyers was a founding member of the Congressional Black Caucus and a longtime civil rights activist. Although minority legislators made up only 25 percent of the committee membership, they represented 43 percent of the Democratic membership on the committee.

Black and Latino members were also represented on the subcommittees of the full committee. House Judiciary has a subcommittee pertaining to immigration and citizenship, as well as a subcommittee on the constitution and civil rights. Black and Latino members accounted for 37.5 percent of all subcommittee members and 60 percent of Democrats on the

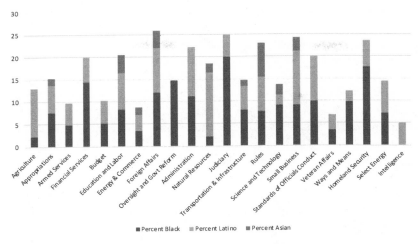

30

25

20

15

10

5

0

■ Percent Black   ■ Percent Latino   ■ Percent Asian

4.1. Racial and Ethnic Composition of House Committees, 110th Congress (2007–2008)

Immigration, Citizenship, Refugees, Border Security, and International Law Subcommittee. Black members accounted 38 percent of the Constitution, Civil Rights, and Civil Liberties Subcommittee, representing 62.5 percent of the Democrats on the subcommittee. There were no Latinos on the subcommittee. Black and Latino legislators also chaired two of the five House Judiciary subcommittees. Thus, in the 2007–2010 period, civil rights organizations possessed a formidable group of legislative advocates capable of steering and influencing the legislative agenda in this crucial policy area.

As figure 4.1 indicates, House Financial Services—whose scope does not make it one of the most likely committees to address civil rights issue—is one of the most diverse committees in the chamber.[7] In the 111th Congress, the committee was 19.9 percent minority, with 14.2 percent black membership, 5.7 percent Latino membership, and no Asian American members. The CBC has coverage on all committees. Black legislators have also increased their presence on one of the prestige committees, the House Ways and Means Committee. Ways and Means is the primary committee responsible for tax policy and for approving governmental spending. In 1975, minorities accounted for 10 percent of Ways and Means membership, which was 7.5 percent black and 2.5 percent Asian American. (There were no Latino members.) By 2007, black legislators had increased their representation on the committee to comprise 9.7 percent of membership. Latinos and Asian Americans are still underrepresented on these prestige committees in comparison to their overall membership in Congress. Asian Americans accounted for only 2.4 percent of Ways and Means membership in 2007, and there were still no Latinos on the committee.

Nonetheless, the overall picture for minority committee representation was, across the board, a vast improvement under Speaker Pelosi compared to what it had been in the 1970s. But representation does not necessarily lead to action, particularly given that black and Latino legislators were, in almost every case, in the minority on the committees and subcommittees on which they sat. The next section examines what happened when bills of interest to minority civil rights organizations were referred to committees, contrasting the post–civil rights era to the Pelosi era in order to determine whether improved committee diversity led to measurable gains for civil rights organizations.

Committee Attention to Bills Lobbied on by Civil Rights Organizations

The remainder of this chapter presents the first part of a two-part analysis of the legislative success of civil rights organizations in Congress. Using data on bill introductions for the 110th Congress (2007–2008) and 111th Congress (2009–2010), I examine whether efforts by civil rights organizations to increase the proportion of black and Latino legislators, or legislative advocates, led to greater legislative success for these organizations' policy initiatives in the House.[8] "Legislative success" is defined for the purpose of this chapter's analysis as the proportion of bills lobbied on by the NAACP, UnidosUS, and LCCR that received a committee markup, or committee action. Committee action was coded 1 if the bill received a committee markup, the source of which was the Library of Congress's database Congress.gov.

Markups are only one of many activities that are important in the multitiered lawmaking process (Smith 2000; Volden and Wiseman 2014). Here, I use committee markup as a measure of legislative success because, first, legislators themselves believe that committee action is a crucial initial step toward achieving their goals (Gamble 2007; Hall 1996; Minta 2011; Krutz 2005). Markup is a difficult hurdle to clear: most bills die in committee.[9] Given the vast disparity between the number of bills introduced each session and the extraordinarily limited set of laws that result—as well as the countless ways in which the national political, cultural, and economic climate affects this outcome—it is essential to identify a more robust way to measure the success of civil rights groups than simply counting the number of bills on their policy agenda that become law in a given session. Markups are effective, moreover, in giving Congress and interest groups an opportunity to draw attention to important issues. Even if a bill does not become a law, markups, along with committee hearings (analyzed in the next chapter), give interest groups and their legislative advocates an opportunity to provide information to Congress about policy concerns. The appendix provides more detail about the methods used to gather and analyze the data that informs this chapter's analysis.

The issues to which civil rights organizations devote their lobbying efforts appear before committees with jurisdictions ranging from agricultural issues to tax policy. Figure 4.2 shows the House committees to which civil rights interest bills were referred in the 110th Congress. As expected, the largest number of bills appeared before House Judiciary. This was true for the NAACP and the LCCR in both the 110th and 111th Congresses. In the 110th Congress, 21 percent of the 143 bills lobbied on by the NAACP and 27.5 percent of the bills lobbied on by the LCCR appeared before House Judiciary. In the 111th Congress, 18.7 percent of the 209 bills lobbied on by the NAACP and 28.6 percent of the 70 bills lobbied on by the LCCR appeared before House Judiciary.[10] Bills referred to House Judiciary supported major policy priorities of the NAACP, such as reducing sentencing disparities between crack and powder cocaine and supporting stricter laws to prohibit racial profiling by law enforcement. House Education and Labor was the second greatest recipient of bills of interest to the NAACP, with

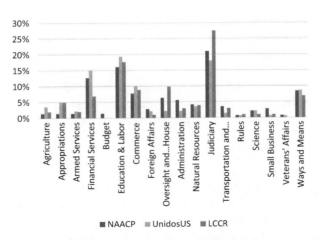

4.2. Percentage of Black and Latino Civil Rights Groups Bill Lobbying Activity by Committee, 110th Congress (2007–2008)

16 percent of NAACP-supported bills appearing before it and 11.4 percent of LCCR bills appearing before the committee in the 110th Congress.

In the 110th and 111th Congresses, the top policy priorities of UnidosUS were immigration reform and education. House Education and Labor is responsible for overseeing immigration and education policy, as well as other labor issues. Not surprisingly, UnidosUS lobbied most on bills that appeared before this committee, with 19 percent of its lobbying agenda appearing before House Education and Labor in the 110th Congress and 14.7 percent in the 111th Congress. House Judiciary was a close second, with 18 percent of the 139 bills lobbied on by UnidosUS in the 110th Congress and 12.8 percent in the 111th Congress.

The bills of most interest to civil rights groups were referred to committees with the greatest diversity. This is not surprising, given that members of Congress try to select committees that have jurisdictions that provide benefits to their constituents. As shown in figure 4.1, House Judiciary had the second highest proportion of black and Latino legislators on the committee, at 25 percent in the 110th Congress. House Education and Labor was also diverse, with 20 percent minority representation, of which 16 percent of members were black and Latino, in the same Congress.

Civil rights organizations experienced success in having their policy initiatives addressed by Congress under the Speaker Pelosi–led House. In the 110th Congress, the committee markup rate was 25.6 percent for all bills lobbied on by the NAACP, 23.9 percent for bills lobbied on by UnidosUS, and 20.1 percent for bills lobbied on by the LCCR. These markup rates were higher than the overall markup rate of 11.2 percent for the 7,215 bills referred to House committees. Bills supported by civil rights groups also had greater hearings rates than other bills that came before the committees. In the 110th Congress, 13 percent of the bills lobbied on by the NAACP, 10.5 percent lobbied on by LCCR, and 9 percent lobbied on by UnidosUS received hearings, in contrast to the overall rate of 6.7 percent for the 7,215 bills referred to House committees.[11]

Under the leadership of House Judiciary Committee chair Rep. John Conyers, civil rights organizations had considerable success with bills that appeared before the committee. In the 110th Congress, House Judiciary held markups on 23 percent of NAACP-supported bills, 20 percent of UnidosUS bills, and 17.8 percent of LCCR bills. This markup rate is higher than the general rate of 12.5 percent for the 885 bills referred to the committee. The hearing rate for NAACP bills was 16.6 percent; for UnidosUS bills, 12 percent; and for LCCR bills, 14.2 percent—again, higher than the hearing rate of 7.8 percent for all bills referred to the committee. Despite partisan polarization, the diverse and liberal Democratic-controlled committee held markups on bills that garnered bipartisan support. Democrats worked with the GOP to pass HR 923, which established the Unsolved Crimes Section in the Civil Rights Division of the Department of Justice and Office of the FBI. Many other groups, such as the LCCR, ACLU, and National Fraternal Order of Police, also lobbied on this bill. Eventually, the bill gained bipartisan support and was signed into law by President Bush. The NAACP focused its attention not just on domestic issues but also on international issues. The committee held a hearing on a bill (HR 5690) that exempted the African National Congress from being considered a terrorist organization. John Conyers was an antiapartheid advocate, and members of the committee served on the CBC's International Affairs Taskforce. House Judiciary also has a subcommittee that addresses international issues. Another bill, HR 1593, reauthorized grant programs for reentry of offenders. More than twenty-five organizations lobbied on the bill, including the Open Society Policy Center, founded in 2008 and funded by George Soros. The bill not only received committee action but also became law—an outcome with a likelihood of only 3 percent.

Although the largest proportion of bills lobbied on by the NAACP, LCCR, and UnidosUS appeared before House Judiciary and House Education and Labor, the committee in which they achieved the most success was House Financial Services. Financial Services ranked third among committees that considered bills of interest to the NAACP, LCCR, and UnidosUS. This is not surprising, considering that the salience of the economic recession and housing crisis of the mid- to late 2000s brought issues such as predatory lending in the housing market to the forefront of the nation's attention. Under the direction of the House Financial Services chairman Rep. Barney Frank (D-MA), the committee brought attention to the economic issues plaguing minority communities. The bills that came before House Financial Services addressed tightening restrictions on payday lenders in minority communities and providing relief to individuals in danger of losing their homes to bank foreclosure. The committee held hearings or markups regarding eliminating predatory lending and on many of the civil rights groups' legislative priorities. Figure 4.3 shows that of the eighteen NAACP bills of interest that appeared before the committee, 61 percent received a markup, and 27 percent received a hearing. UnidosUS was equally successful, with 57.1 percent of the twenty-one bills it supported receiving a committee markup and 19 percent receiving a hearing. The LCCR, too, was successful lobbying before this committee, with 85.7 percent of seven bills lobbied on receiving a markup and 28.5 percent receiving a hearing.

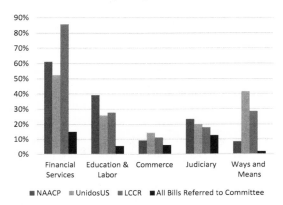

4.3. Markup Success Rate for Bills Lobbied on by Civil Rights Organizations, 110th Congress (2007–2008)

The markup and hearing success rates of NAACP, UnidosUS, and LCCR bills were higher than the 15 percent markup average for the 477 bills referred to Financial Services, as well as the hearing average of 5.6 percent. The NAACP, UnidosUS, and the LCCR all lobbied on the anti–predatory lending bill, and Rep. Maxine Waters (D-CA) worked closely with these groups. Waters is a longtime member of the committee and also a member of the Congressional Black Caucus, and she chaired the CBC's Housing Task Force. NAACP lobbyist Hilary Shelton testified at hearings in support of enacting tougher laws against predatory lenders. UnidosUS lobbyist Charles Kamasaki testified at hearings regarding providing relief to Latinos from foreclosures. In an era of political party polarization, the committee members worked to get these measures passed. HR 2895 would establish a national housing trust fund. Rep. Frank delegated the chairing of the hearing to Rep. Waters.

Civil rights groups' success was not just confined to the area of housing; it also extended to other policy areas and committees that had responsibility over those areas. In the 110th Congress, the NAACP and UnidosUS spent significant time lobbying on issues that appeared before House Education and Labor. The committee held markups on 39 percent of NAACP-supported bills and 26 percent of UnidosUS bills. This was higher than the overall markup average of 5 percent for 701 bills referred to this committee, as well as the House chamber average of 6.7 percent.[12] More astounding is that 26 percent of the bills supported by the NAACP and UnidosUS became public law—well above the House average of 4 percent. UnidosUS spent significant time lobbying on the Development, Relief, and Education for Alien Minors (DREAM) Act and other immigration-related issues. Although Democrats and Republicans supported immigration reform, they did not agree on the solution. UnidosUS, the NAACP, and the LCCR supported passage of the DREAM Act. They also lobbied on HR 1338, the Paycheck Fairness Act.

Civil rights organizations were similarly successful during the 111th Congress following the election of President Obama. The committee markup rate on all bills lobbied by each group was 18.2 percent for the NAACP and 18.4 percent for UnidosUS. This overall markup rate in the 110th Congress was much better than for the 111th Congress, and, not surprisingly, the bill passage rate was also better. Bills received more markup action when minorities had a voice, and they were also more likely to become law. The NAACP had a high rate of success with the House Armed Services, Small Business, and Science committees, although these committees combined represented only 3.3 percent of the NAACP's lobbying agenda, which was dominated by House Judiciary, Education and Labor, and Financial Services (figure 4.4). Civil rights groups had approximately the same level of success with these committees as they did under the 110th Congress. The combined committee markup rate for House bills (bills with the HR designation only or bills that substantively make new law or amend existing law) was 11 percent in the 110th Congress, compared to 9 percent committee markup success in the 111th Congress.

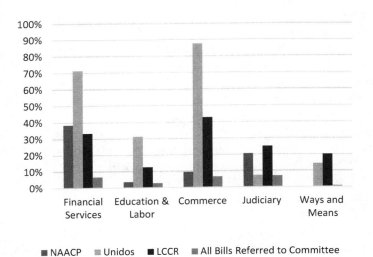

4.4. Markup Success Rate for Bills Lobbied on by Civil Rights Organizations, 111th Congress (2009–2010)

Of course, many factors beyond the presence of minority legislators might affect the success of civil rights organizations in advancing their policy agenda in committee. Committee chairs are usually charged with sponsoring major legislation that comes before their committees. The committee chair has the ability to set the agenda and determine which bills receive hearings or markups. The committee chair also has the resources of committee staff to devote attention to these issues. Cosponsorship of bills by many legislators can increase the chance of a bill receiving committee action; more cosponsors demonstrate a bill has gained significant support among legislators, as legislators who cosponsor a bill are attaching their reputation to that legislation. Bills with few cosponsors have little support or are in the beginning stages of gaining legislative support. Thus, although civil rights organizations were successful in the 110th and 111th Congresses, it is unclear how much of this success can be directly attributed to the racial and ethnic diversity of legislators. The next sections drill down into the question of whether the presence of black and Latino legislators in the House can be isolated as an important factor in the lobbying success of black American and Latino civil rights organizations.

Legislative Success of Civil Rights Groups Representing Black Interests

The presence of black legislators contributes significantly to the legislative success of the NAACP and the LCCR—the two groups that spend the most time and resources lobbying the federal government on behalf of black American interests. Tables 4.1 and 4.2 show that even when accounting for factors such as ideology of committee members and committee jurisdiction, bills lobbied on by the NAACP and LCCR were more likely to receive markup in committees that had a higher proportion of black members than in committees with fewer black legislators.[13]

Figures 4.5 and 4.6 illustrate the significant effect that legislative advocates exerted in drawing attention to the legislative priorities of the NAACP, such as drug-related sentencing disparities, equal pay for women, and anti–predatory lending legislation, in the 110th and 111th Congresses.[14] In the 110th Congress, when a committee was 11 percent black—the overall committee average—the likelihood of a committee markup of NAACP-supported legislation was 0.17, but when the proportion of black legislators increased to 20 percent, the probability of legislative success was bolstered to 0.85. Conversely, the chance of markup action almost disappeared, at 0.01, when blacks accounted for only 5 percent of a committee

Table 4.1. Likelihood of Markup Action on Bills Supported by Civil Rights
Organizations, House, 110th Congress (2007–2008)

Explanatory variables	NAACP	UnidosUS	LCCR
Committee level			
Proportion of Black members	22.36**	7.01*	11.63**
	(4.61)	(3.23)	(4.91)
Proportion of Latino members	8.08**	5.60	2.87
	(4.01)	(4.40)	(4.15)
Proportion of women members	11.55**	−4.90*	−.865
	(2.52)	(2.37)	(2.93)
Median committee ideology	2.61**	.402	−.208
	(1.01)	(.920)	(.973)
Committee chair and bill sponsor	.947*	1.25**	1.14+
	(.467)	(.427)	(.657)
Race and ethnic minority committee chair	.698	−.172	−.286
	(.483)	(.352)	(.488)
House Judiciary Committee	−2.43**	−.544	−1.14*
	(.701)	(.474)	(.563)
Individual level			
Black bill sponsor	.072	.784*	.927*
	(.334)	(.352)	(.482)
Latino bill sponsor	−1.18+	−.721	—
	(.662)	(.461)	
Women bill sponsor	-.322	.339	.502
	(.382)	(.391)	(.441)
Number of cosponsors	.005**	.005*	.006*
	(.002)	(.002)	(.003)
Chamber seniority of bill sponsor	−.080**	.012	.013
	(.028)	(.030)	(.032)
Constant	−4.47**	−1.60*	−3.14**
	(.896)	(.728)	(.830)
Log pseudo-likelihood	−60.94	−56.81	−39.26
Wald chi-square	47.09	49.94	23.36
Pseudo-R^2	.257	.273	.250
N	144	142	104

Note: Robust standard errors are in parentheses.
*p < .05 (two-tailed). **p <.01 (two-tailed). +p < .10 (two-tailed).

(see figure 4.5). The impact of race on predicting committee action on a bill was significant even when committees were filled with members who were preference outliers or had liberal voting records. The average median ideology score of committees where NAACP-supported bills appeared was −0.194 in the 110th Congress. The liberalness of the committee did not seem to affect the likelihood of a markup by the committee. Even on committees with prominent liberals and supporters of civil rights, such as Rep. Zoe Lofgren (D-CA) and Rep. Adam Schiff (D-CA) on House Judiciary, or House Financial Services with Rep. Barney Frank (D-MA) and Rep. Steve

Table 4.2. Likelihood of Markup Action on Bills Supported by Civil Rights Organizations, House, 111th Congress (2009–2010)

Explanatory variables	NAACP	UnidosUS	LCCR
Committee level			
Proportion of black members	5.31⁺	6.68	17.33*
	(3.04)	(5.15)	(8.20)
Proportion of Latino members	.990	−11.03	−83.92
	(6.42)	(6.81)	(43.58)
Proportion of women members	4.99⁺	5.44+	−40.27⁺
	(2.85)	(3.14)	(21.07)
Median committee ideology	7.03*	2.50	−25.36
	(2.39)	(3.83)	(18.44)
Committee chair and bill sponsor	1.34**	.638	.228
	(.337)	(.561)	(.570)
Race and ethnic minority committee chair	.220	.005	—
	(.396)	(.543)	
House judiciary committee	.645	.288	5.20**
	(.439)	(.673)	(1.88)
Individual level			
Black bill sponsor	−.012	−.404	−.420*
	(.280)	(.590)	(.526)
Latino bill sponsor	.326	—	—
	(.642)		
Women bill sponsor	−.067	.408	.752
	(.381)	(.524)	(.623)
Number of cosponsors	.000	.005⁺	−.000
	(.002)	(.003)	(.004)
Chamber seniority of bill sponsor	−.062**	.028	.071⁺
	(.023)	(.038)	(.041)
Constant	−.856	−2.27⁺	4.30⁺
	(.865)	(.728)	(2.54)
Log pseudo-likelihood	−66.70	−30.71	−28.05
Wald chi-square	30.97	29.68	20.99
Pseudo-R^2	.170	.160	.199
N	209	99	70

Note: Robust standard errors are in parentheses.

*$p < .05$ (two-tailed). **$p < .01$ (two-tailed). ⁺$p < .10$ (two-tailed).

Cohen (D-TN), the diversity of the committee still mattered. In fact, the committee where the NAACP experienced the most success was House Financial Services, with a median ideology score of −0.07 in the 110th Congress and −0.179 in the 111th Congress, indicating that it was one of the more moderate committees in the sample.

When Democrats gained control of the presidency, the likelihood of finding the racial and ethnic composition of committee membership important might be expected to diminish, as Democrat-backed legislation should have a greater probability of becoming law under a Democratic

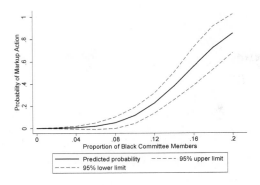

4.5. Black Legislators and House Markup Action on NAACP
Supported Legislation, 110th Congress (2007–2008)

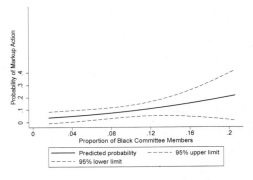

4.6. Black Legislators and House Committee Markup Action on NAACP
Supported Legislation, 111th Congress (2009–2010)

presidency. Although the effect of committees' racial and ethnic composition was not as strong in the 111th Congress as in the 110th Congress,
table 4.2 shows that the proportion of black legislators on committees
continued to be significant in predicting the likelihood of markup on
NAACP-supported bills in the 111th Congress. The predicted probability
of receiving markup was only 0.03 when blacks accounted for 2 percent of
committee membership, but it increased to 0.22 when the committee was
21 percent black (see figure 4.6).

In addition to promoting minority interests related to the financial crisis, civil rights organizations and their legislative advocates were successful in getting Congress to address other civil rights legislation. Sentencing
disparities legislation received committee action in the 110th and 111th
Congresses and eventually became law when President Obama signed it.

Civil rights organizations wanted the sentencing disparity completely eliminated, but legislators agreed to a compromise to get the bill passed. The bill had bipartisan support, and a variety of organized interests lobbied for it, most notably powerful business groups.

The impact of diversity in increasing the probability of success for minority civil rights organizations is not just a function of the issue jurisdiction of committees. Although bills referred to House Judiciary represented a significant portion of the NAACP's and LCCR's lobbying agenda, most bills lobbied on by the NAACP and LCCR were not referred to House Judiciary (see figure 4.2). As shown earlier, black legislators serve on this committee at a much higher rate than on any other committee; however, despite the higher proportion of blacks and the committee's jurisdiction over civil rights and criminal justice issues, the impact of diversity is still significant in determining the success rate of these groups in the 110th and 111th Congresses.

Although Canon (1999) found that sponsorship by black legislators increased the likelihood of a bill becoming law, there is little direct evidence to support the idea that the race or ethnicity of a bill's sponsor increases its chance of committee success when it comes to bills lobbied on by the NAACP and LCCR. Given the variety and vast number of bills that minority civil rights groups lobby on, it is unlikely that black and Latino legislators could sponsor all the bills important to civil rights organizations and minority communities. Civil rights organizations' focus on getting committee chairs to sponsor legislation is a prudent and viable strategy, considering that committee chair sponsorship is found to be the most significant factor in determining whether a bill receives a hearing or markup in the vast majority of the models.

The proportion of Latino legislators was also significant in explaining the success of NAACP-supported bills in the 110th Congress. Figure 4.7 shows that when there were zero Latino legislators on a committee, the probability of a bill receiving committee markup was 0.10. When the proportion of Latinos on the committee increased to 15 percent, then the predicted probability of a bill receiving a markup rose to 0.40. The presence of legislators such as Rep. Luis Gutierrez (D-IL) and Rep. Linda Sanchez (D-CA) increased bills' chances of a markup hearing. Although the presence of Latino legislators was significant when Democrats held the House during the 110th Congress, the proportion of Latino legislators on the committee was not significant in predicting markup success on bills supported by the NAACP during the Obama years, or the 111th Congress.

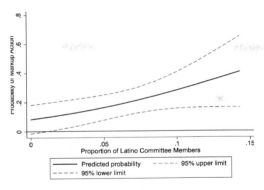

4.7. Latino Legislators and House Markup Action on NAACP Supported
Legislation, 110th Congress (2007–2008)

The LCCR is not strictly a black civil rights organization, but its policy priorities closely mirrored those of the NAACP in the 110th and 111th
Congresses. This is not surprising, because the head of the LCCR during
Pelosi's years as Speaker of the House was Wade Henderson, who had
been the head lobbyist for the NAACP's Washington Bureau in the early
to mid-1990s. The proportion of black legislators on a committee was also
significant in determining whether LCCR bills received a markup. In the
110th Congress, the likelihood that bills lobbied on by the LCCR received
a markup was 0.44 when committee membership was 20 percent black,
compared to 0.01 predicted probability when the committee was 1 percent
black (see figure 4.8). The same was true when Obama was president and
Democrats controlled the House in the 111th Congress: the proportion of
blacks on committees was significant in ensuring that LCCR-supported bills
received attention. Figure 4.9 shows similar results for a bill's chance of
markup, with 0.50 predicted probability of LCCR bills receiving a markup
when blacks represented 21 percent of the committee compared to 0.00
probability when blacks represented 1 percent of committee membership.

When committee chairs sponsor legislation supported by civil rights organizations, then the likelihood of a bill receiving a markup hearing is significant. This is true for both NAACP- and LCCR-supported legislation during the 110th Congress, but it is only true for the NAACP during the 111th
Congress. Although committee chairs are important to civil rights groups'
achieving success, I did not find any support for the hypothesis that the
racial and ethnic background of committee chairs was significant in predicting the likelihood of a markup hearing for NAACP- or LCCR-supported

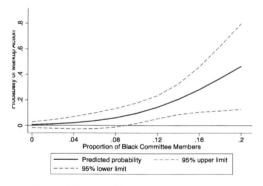

4.8. Black Legislators and House Markup Action on LCCR
Supported Legislation, 110th Congress (2007–2008)

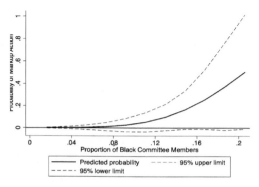

4.9. Black Legislators and Markup Action on LCCR
Supported Legislation, 111th Congress (2009–2010)

legislation in either the 110th or 111th Congresses (see tables 4.1 and 4.2)—a surprising result, given that committee chairs determine whether a bill receives a markup hearing.

Perhaps the most interesting finding is that the presence of women on committees under Pelosi's speakership also increased committee attention to issues championed by the NAACP and LCCR. During the Bush and Pelosi years of the 110th Congress, the proportion of women on committees played a significant role in the success of what were ostensibly minority issues. Bills referred to committees with an average membership of 16 percent women had a 0.17 percent probability of receiving a markup. This probability improved to 0.77 when the proportion of women increased to 31 percent. Thus, diversity is not just about a one-to-one correspondence whereby black legislators' actions only benefit blacks, or women legislators' actions only benefit women (Minta and Sinclair-Chapman 2013). There is significant overlap between women's issues and minority issues (Minta and Brown 2014). This has been the case for many years, but women's rights and minority rights groups usually define issues in a manner that supports their own organizations and constituents. Yet advocacy for civil rights is a collective public good. Although the civil rights advocacy of the 1950s and 1960s focused on gaining rights for black Americans in the South, blacks could not exclude Latinos or women for demanding that they also be included in sharing the protections and benefits that civil rights affords, even if those groups long opposed allying with blacks to gain civil rights protections. Thus, when language provisions were included in the VRA, the NAACP could not stop Latinos from enjoying the benefits of those protections, despite a belief that Latinos were not committed to advancing civil rights. Blacks could not prevent women from demanding that the Equal Employment Opportunity Commission address issues not just of racial discrimination but also of gender discrimination, even though as many white women opposed civil rights for blacks as supported them. Contestation on similar issues at the federal level can lead to gains for multiple groups with dissimilar interests. As chapter 2 showed, Latino groups such as LULAC and the GI Forum did not support civil rights for blacks but pursued a whiteness strategy to gain inclusion for Mexican Americans. The rise of the Chicano movement and the formation of UnidosUS led to collaborative efforts with black interest groups. The NAACP, the SCLC, and other groups produced the VRA and subsequent amendments to the VRA whereby Latinos obtained inclusion under the language-provision amendments.

This point becomes particularly salient in the next section, on the legislative success of civil rights groups representing Latino interests, as the data shows that minority representation on committees did matter for the success of Latino-backed legislation—but it was black representation on committees that made the critical difference, just as Latino representation on committees provided strong support for legislation important to black civil rights organizations.

Legislative Success for Civil Rights Groups Representing Latino Interests

Policy priorities of UnidosUS, such as expanding home ownership and the DREAM (Development, Relief, and Education for Alien Minors) Act, were more likely to receive attention in the 110th and 111th Congresses from

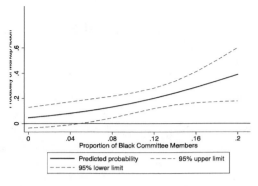

4.10. Black Legislators and Markup Action on UnidosUS Supported
Legislation, 110th Congress (2007–2008)

committees with more racial and ethnic diversity. Interestingly, however, it was the proportion of blacks on committees that was most important in predicting support for UnidosUS's policy priorities. In the 110th Congress, the probability of a committee markup on UnidosUS-supported legislation was 0.05 when there were no black legislators on the committee, compared to probability of 0.37 when the committee was 20 percent black (figure 4.10). The racial diversity of the committee did not have a direct effect on whether UnidosUS-supported legislation received a committee markup in the 111th Congress.

Surprisingly, the proportion of Latinos on committees did not have a direct effect on the probability of committee action on UnidosUS policy priorities. The conflict that once defined the relationship between black and Latino groups from the 1920s to the 1960s diminished significantly in the 2000s. In a comprehensive examination of black and Latino civil rights groups at the national level, Hero and Preuhs (2013) found that the groups work in different policy domains, in neither coalition nor conflict. The racial diversity of legislators in Congress is beneficial to both black and Latino groups. Members of Congress have formed their own coalitions like the Congressional Tri-Caucus to address issues that are common to black, Latino, and Asian American groups. Many of the issues that UnidosUS lobbied on were also considered important and close to the policy space of blacks. In fact, Hero and Preuhs (2013) found that black legislators were likely to support the National Hispanic Leadership Agenda issues featured on the NHLA's voting scorecards. Latino legislators were supportive of the same issues, but they did not stand out from black or white legislators on these issues. Moreover, more than 29 percent of UnidosUS's agenda significantly overlaps with NAACP agenda items that come before the House Judiciary Committee and the Education and Labor Committee. Many of the issues lobbied on by UnidosUS are also broadly supported by blacks, women, and Democrats.

The fact that black legislators are supportive of Latino interests is not new or unusual. In the 1970s, during the reauthorization of the Voting Rights Act, CBC members supported the inclusion of the language-provision requirements even though the NAACP's main lobbyist, Clarence Mitchell, opposed their inclusion and instead advocated for their inclusion in a separate bill; the NAACP also provided the veto that kept the LCCR from supporting the language provisions. Despite the opposition of the NAACP, black legislators supported the inclusion of the language requirements. CBC members also supported the reauthorization of the language provisions in the 102nd Congress—HR 4312, the Voting Rights Language Assistance Act, was introduced by Rep. José Serrano (D-NY) and cosponsored by CBC chair Rep. Ed Towns (D-NY) and other CBC members—as well as the immigration reform efforts of UnidosUS. Even on immigration, where the position of UnidosUS is distinct from that of most other civil rights groups, black members of Congress and white Democrats have been just as supportive of UnidosUS's policy agenda as Latino legislators have. Moreover, the NAACP and UnidosUS advocate on issues that include more than civil rights—although the NAACP spends more time on traditional civil rights issues than UnidosUS. The focus on government operations consumes a large proportion of the lobbying time of both groups, and in the case of UnidosUS, this means devoting time to securing funding for its affiliates.

Immigration reform was one of many issues of importance to Latino civil rights organizations, but even under a unified Democratic congress, the bill did not go anywhere. Diversity in Congress was beneficial to other issues lobbied on by UnidosUS, however. In the 110th Congress, the group lobbied on bills such as the Improving Head Start for School Readiness Act of 2007 (HR 1429) and the Health Equity and Accountability Act of 2007 (HR 3014).

Sponsorship of bills by black or Latino legislators did not predict greater success in terms of committee markup. During the 110th Congress, the result was significant, but not in the 111th Congress. Black bill sponsorship was important, but Latino bill sponsorship was not. The presence of minority chairs on committees was likewise not significant in explaining the likelihood of a markup in either the 110th or the 111th Congress.

Conclusion

This chapter has shown racial and ethnic diversity in Congress to be a key determinant in explaining the success of the bills on which civil rights organizations lobby Congress. Polarization on congressional committees does not diminish the level of civil rights groups' success when Democrats control the House. Even in the divided environment of the 110th Congress under President George W. Bush, civil rights organizations were successful in getting Congress to pay attention to their issues in committees as measured through markup rates on bills supported by civil rights organizations. The success of civil rights groups in Congress cannot be explained in terms of who spends the most on lobbying or who contributes the most money to political candidates. Instead, diversity on legislative committees explains why civil rights groups are successful beyond these traditional measures of influence. Minority members of Congress acted as advocates for civil rights policy in the 110th and 111th Congresses by drawing attention to bills through markups. Although having a minority sponsor did not increase the probability of markup on a given bill—nor did the presence of minority committee chairs—increased racial and ethnic diversity on committees did. Not only were civil rights organizations successful with committees that have jurisdiction over civil rights, such as House Judiciary, they were also successful in other policy dimensions.

As have other scholars, I find that the positive effects of legislative diversity go well beyond a legislator's direct representation of his or her own racial and ethnic co-constituents: groups with overlapping agendas can play a significant role in pushing for the issues that are important to other minorities, and even to marginalized white voters. The presence of black legislators has played a particularly significant role in drawing attention to the concerns of UnidosUS even when the proportion of Latinos on committees was not significant. The NAACP's agenda is a more traditional civil rights agenda, concerned with fighting discrimination in housing and employment. UnidosUS's lobbying agenda contains less of these issues; however, UnidosUS also benefits from committee diversity.

Minta and Sinclair-Chapman (2013) found that diversity was important in explaining the increase in congressional attention to civil rights and social welfare issues from 1951 through 2006. They did not examine, however, whether diversity on congressional committees was the main causal factor for committee action on minority issues, nor did they examine the committee success of issues lobbied on by civil rights organizations. Thus, I provide in this chapter a first step to understanding the role committees play in drawing attention to the policy priorities of civil rights groups. An increase in diversity on committees results in more success for civil rights groups in the legislative arena. Diversity of membership on House committees has played a significant role in increasing the legislative success of black and Latino advocacy groups. Minority legislators are vital to providing voices to these groups in committee markup of important bills and at congressional hearings.

Limitations on campaign contributions and lobbying for 501(c)(3) organizations make it difficult to assess the impact of these organizations on the congressional agenda. This study has argued that interest groups, particularly civil rights organizations, obtain access to members of Congress by other means—perhaps making up for their resource disadvantages. This chapter has analyzed rates of committee markup on bills supported by civil rights organizations to demonstrate the impressive efficacy of that strategy.

This chapter's findings also contribute to the debate about the effectiveness of majority-minority districts by measuring whether the presence of more racial and ethnic minorities changes the outputs of Congress. Few studies make the link between how the diversity of the legislature contributes to interest group policy success. Scholars usually measure whether individual legislators are responsive to their constituents, not whether civil rights organizations are effective in representing minority interests at the federal level. Increasing diversity in committee membership enhances the prospects of bills supported by civil rights organizations. The strategy of creating more minority districts has been beneficial to interest group advocacy overall. Thus, liberal and conservative critiques, such as that from Lani Guinier and Carol Swain, that descriptive representatives will have little success in Congress are not entirely accurate. Black electoral success has led directly to the enhanced success of minority interest groups at the federal level.

Appendix

Measuring Legislative Success

To test whether diversity on committees leads to legislative success, I examined the likelihood that the bills supported and lobbied on by the NAACP, UnidosUS, and LCCR received committee action in the U.S. House of Representatives.[15] Using data on bill introductions for the 110th Congress (2007–2008) and the 111th Congress (2009–2010), I examined whether redistricting efforts by civil rights organizations to increase the proportion of African American and Latino legislators, or legislative advocates, has led to these organizations' greater legislative success in Congress. I employed a bill committee match to estimate this likelihood of committee action. Again, legislative success was defined as the proportion of bills lobbied on by the NAACP, LCCR, and UnidosUS that advance successfully in Congress.[16] Specifically, I examined how far these bills have advanced in the legislative process in terms of receiving a committee markup session. The committee markup variable was coded as 1 if the bill received a markup session and 0 if it did not. The committee markup data were obtained from the Library of Congress's website Congress.gov.

Because bills may be referred to multiple committees, the unit of analysis is a bill-committee match. For example, in the 110th Congress, the antidiscrimination bill, HR 2015, by Rep. Barney Frank was referred to multiple committees in the House: Education and Labor, Oversight and Government Reform, and House Administration. Thus, the same bill is counted as three separate observations in order to estimate the likelihood of the three committees holding a markup. I use probit to estimate the likelihood of committee action given the committee's diversity.

The primary source of bill-lobbying activity by civil rights groups was obtained from the Center for Responsive Politics. The organization collects data from financial reports that groups are required to file under the Lobbying Disclosure Act of 1995. The act requires that groups report how much money they spend on lobbying, the specific bills on which they lobby, and the governmental entities they lobby. Although the LDRs provide some details on organizations' lobbying activity, these reports can understate the advocacy efforts groups devote to given issues. First, groups do not have to register if they fail to reach a certain threshold. Nonprofits with $5,000 in annual income are required to register with the IRS. Only groups with greater than or equal to $25,000 in income are required to file a tax return (Berry and Arons 2003).

The law is limited in terms of its definition of what constitutes lobbying activity. Moreover, groups do not always report on what issues they have lobbied on, and sometimes they might understate the amount of time they have spent on lobbying. Also, LDRs do not allow for measurement of how often civil rights groups met with legislators or executive branch officials. In considering these sources of inaccuracy, it is important to remember that nonprofit groups are far more likely to understate than to overstate their advocacy, as a result of the fear of losing 501(c)(3) status for spending too many resources on lobbying.

In determining whether groups lobbied on an issue, I use LDRs for the 110th and 111th Congresses to define the issues, which are self-reported by the groups. The LDA gives a narrow definition of lobbying activity (Baumgartner et al. 2009). First, only groups spending at least $20,000 on lobbying during any six-month period must register with each chamber as a lobbying organization. Grassroots lobbying, such as action alerts urging the groups' members to contact members of Congress, testimony at public hearings, or providing comment to agencies during the rulemaking process, is not considered lobbying activity.

Once the bills that groups lobbied on were identified, I gathered additional information about the disposition of the bills from the online Congressional Bills Project database.[17] The database includes current and historical information on all bills introduced in Congress from 1946 through 2011. The bills in the Congressional Bills database are categorized into 19 major and 225 minor topic content codes that range from macroeconomics to transportation. The Congressional Bills database also lists the legislators who sponsored and cosponsored the legislation, as well as the final disposition of each bill by the committee and chamber, and whether the president signed the bill into law.

Although the primary variables of interest are the proportion of minority legislators serving on congressional committees, I included several control variables, such as whether a committee had a minority representative as its chair, whether the sponsor of the bill was also the chair of the committee, and whether the sponsor was both a racial/ethnic minority and committee chair. I expected the same positive relationship when the sponsor had a high seniority score in the chamber.

Moreover, I control for the number of cosponsors of a bill, as an increased value would signal greater support for a bill, which could increase the likelihood of a bill's receiving committee action. The ideological composition of the committee can also have an impact on the success of civil rights bills in committee; this is proxied by including in the model the committee median of first-dimension DW-NOMINATE scores. A more liberal committee will invest more resources in civil rights bills. Finally, to control for the possibility that bill sponsors are acting in accordance with their constituents' preferences, I used a common proxy for district preferences— district demographics. Specifically, one variable is the percentage of black voting-age constituents and another is the percentage of Latino voting-age constituents in the sponsor's district. Previous research has found that bills sponsored by minority legislators were more successful in advancing in the legislative process than those sponsored by whites (Canon 1999). I controlled for the effects of gender by including variables that account for whether the bill sponsor is female and the percentage of women in committee. Last, I controlled for the House Judiciary Committee—the committee with primary jurisdiction on civil rights enforcement and criminal justice issues.

FIVE

Inviting Friends to Testify

In the 1930s, the executive secretary of the NAACP, Charles Houston, testified before congressional committees regarding the proposed Social Security Act (SSA) of 1935.[1] He argued that provisions of the bill denying benefit eligibility to agricultural and domestic workers discriminated against the black community, because blacks were disproportionately concentrated in those employment categories. Houston urged Congress to amend the SSA bill to include agricultural and domestic workers so that black workers would have the same access as white workers to a guaranteed retirement income and disability benefits. He argued that if agricultural and domestic workers were excluded from the entitlement program, they would have to seek relief from means-based programs—and that benefit eligibility for these programs was determined by state government officials who opposed providing relief to blacks. Specifically, Southern Democrats opposed including blacks because doing so would challenge the racial caste system in the South. Northern Democrats and President Franklin Roosevelt avoided this issue because they did not want to lose the support of Southern Democrats, who were important to the success of Roosevelt's New Deal relief programs.

Although the NAACP was not successful in getting Congress to include agricultural and domestic workers under the umbrella of the SSA, the group was provided a rare opportunity to testify before lawmakers about the impact of proposed legislation on minority constituents in the context of Southern Democrats' opposition, which limited the NAACP's testimony opportunities. From 1909 through 1950, before the civil rights movement, the NAACP testified before House committees 133 times, or an average of three times per year.[2] The migration of blacks to the North and their incorporation into the Democratic Party political machines in places such as

Chicago and New York, along with civil rights protests in the South, led to the passage of major civil rights legislation. Since the passage of the Civil Rights Act of 1964 and the Voting Rights Act of 1965, representatives of the NAACP have testified more frequently: from 1966 through 2014, the NAACP testified 533 times, or an average of 11 times per year. Other civil rights organizations have also emerged to testify regularly before Congress, including UnidosUS, MALDEF, and the LCCR. These groups have become valuable voices in policy making—mainly on racial or ethnic issues, although they have also expanded their reach beyond civil rights.

As minority civil rights groups testified more frequently before committees, so did minority legislators. In the 1950s, Rep. Adam Clayton Powell Jr. (D-NY), the primary congressional champion for the legislative agenda of civil rights organizations (Hamilton 1991), testified before many House committees that addressed issues of importance to blacks. He chaired the House Education and Labor Committee and held hearings on civil rights and other issues affecting the black community. In the 2010s, however, the NAACP no longer had to rely solely on one legislator to champion its legislative agenda. Black legislators, particularly those who are members of the CBC, had become major advocates in congressional testimony supporting legislation affecting black Americans. Latino legislators, including those who are members of the CHC, similarly represent the interests of Latinos through congressional testimony.

This chapter extends chapter 4's examination of the extent to which diversity in House membership was important to the legislative success of minority civil rights organizations. Again, I consider whether civil rights organizations achieved greater legislative success as a result of higher levels of minority representation in the House, as well as inquiring into whether political polarization and shifts in party control of the House affected this success. Here, however, I am interested in congressional testimony before committees rather than in markup sessions as a measure of civil rights organizations' legislative success. Taken together, both chapters provide a measure at civil rights organizations' influence in Congress through their alliance with minority legislative advocates.

I begin with a close look at whether representatives of minority civil rights organizations testify in areas identified by blacks and Latinos as top priorities, such as the issues of economy, health care, immigration, and race. Next, I measure whether the presence of more blacks and Latinos in the House leads to more opportunities for minority interest groups to testify at hearings. I then examine the frequency and substance of black and Latino legislators' testimony in minority-interest areas and to what extent they supplement or complement the advocacy efforts of civil rights organizations. Finally, I focus on whether growing polarization in the House limits the ability of interest groups to testify before House committees.

I find that increasing numbers of minority legislators in Congress has given civil rights organizations such as UnidosUS, MALDEF, the LCCR, and the NAACP more opportunities to testify at hearings, even controlling for the overall increase in the number of House hearings. Not only are the representatives of these groups testifying more frequently, but the CBC and CHC have joined them in providing a high level of advocacy for minority interests in ways that are both supplementary and complementary. That is, civil rights groups' strategy of increasing the number of legislative advocates in Congress has succeeded in giving them more opportunities to push for their policy priorities—and to have those priorities advanced by legislative advocates. Despite the increased volume of testimony by minority rights groups, however, I also find that rising polarization and GOP control do limit the testimony opportunities granted to some civil rights organizations.

Witness Testimony by Civil Rights Organizations

Testifying at hearings—a more visible form of advocacy than lobbying—provides civil rights groups and legislators with an opportunity to represent their groups and constituent interests. Citizen groups use witness testimony as a tool of advocacy more than do business organizations, professional associations, and unions (Berry 1999). The chairs of House committees invite advocacy groups to testify on proposed legislation and matters relating to implementing policies at federal agencies. Representatives of groups provide information regarding the potential impact of the proposed legislation on their members or those they represent. Because not all groups are invited to testify, civil rights organizations work to establish a reputation with members of Congress that permits them to increase these opportunities. Advocacy organizations provide legislators with valuable information about the needs and wants of their constituents, which can improve the electoral chances of these legislators (Hansen 1991) or help the chamber make good public policy (Fenno 1978; Krehbiel 1991).

Witness testimony, unlike lobbying, is a constrained activity. Congress must first decide to hold a hearing on an issue of relevance to civil rights groups. Specifically, this decision falls to the committee chair. The chair of the committee usually consults with the ranking minority member of the committee as well as with rank-and-file members who serve on the committee. They might also consult with majority-party leadership and party caucuses. As black and Latino legislators constitute a greater share than they once did of the Democratic Party delegation, these groups gain more influence on which hearings are held and who is invited to testify (Minta and Sinclair-Chapman 2013).

The total number of hearings held by Congress in each session has steadily risen since the New Deal, when Congress began expanding its power to regulate the economy and, later, when it assumed a greater role in addressing environmental concerns, workplace safety, and civil rights. The 61st Congress (1909–1911) held only 726 hearings: 559 in the House and 167 in the Senate. By the 113th Congress (2013–14), hearings had increased substantially to a total of 2,581: 1,268 in the House and 1,313 in the Senate.[3] In the area of racial and ethnic civil rights, the House held an average of 2.4 hearings on civil rights per Congress from the 61st through the 81st Congresses (1909–1950), compared to an average of 16.6 hearings on civil rights per Congress from the 82nd through the 113th Congress (1951–2014).[4]

As hearings increased in frequency, so did opportunities for groups to testify. The three oldest civil rights organizations, the NAACP, the NUL, and LULAC, all testified more post-VRA in the 90th through 113th Congresses (1967–2014) than they had pre-VRA in the 61st through 89th Congresses (1909–1966). The NAACP testified an average of 12.1 times per session in the post-VRA era, compared to only 3.6 times in the pre-VRA era (figure 5.1).[5] The high point of NAACP testimony occurred between 1971 and 1986, when the group testified an average of 20.1 times per congressional term. The low point occurred from the 61st to 76th Congresses (1909–1940), with an average of 1.06 instances of testimony per congressional term and a total of only 17 instances over the period. The nature of NAACP testimony has ranged from encouraging Congress to enact antilynching legislation in the 1950s to supporting the elimination of racial discrimination in employment and lending in the 2010s. The NUL testified an average of 0.92 times per session, or 26 times total, in the pre-VRA era, compared to an average of 5.1 times per session, or 122 times, in the post-VRA era.

Two of the three major Latino civil rights organizations, UnidosUS and MALDEF, were founded in 1968, and LULAC did not testify at all prior to that time, making comparison of Latino organizations' pre-VRA and post-VRA testimony rates impossible. As established experts on the needs of the Latino community, however, these organizations' representatives are regularly invited to testify before committees. From 82nd through the 113th Congress (1968–2014), UnidosUS testified the most frequently of

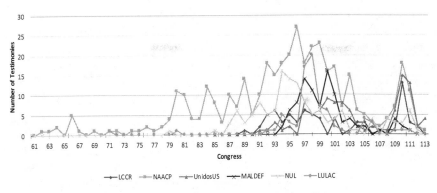

5.1. House Testimony by Black and Latino Interest Groups,
61st–114th Congress (1909–2014)

any Latino group, at 105 times, compared to 93 for MALDEF and 77 for
LULAC. Moreover, the frequency with which these groups are called to testify before the House has increased. In the early years of UnidosUS, from
1971 through 1980, the group testified an average of 1.4 times per session,
but from the 92nd through the 96th Congress (1981–1990), this number
increased to 7.2 times per session.

    Although representatives of civil rights groups testify more today than
they did in the immediate post-VRA era, to what extent are they representing the interests of black and Latino interests in Congress? In chapter 3,
I found that black and Latino civil rights groups' lobbying efforts did a
good job of representing black and Latino group interests. The next section
examines minority advocacy groups' responsiveness to black and Latino
interests at congressional hearings.

Responsiveness to Black Interests

Black Americans rank racial issues, social welfare, and jobs as top legislative priorities. I find that civil rights groups effectively represent minority
interests in their witness testimony activity. From 1951 to 2014, the NAACP
spent 34 percent of its testimony time testifying on civil rights issues before House committees (figure 5.2). The timing of this testimony has been
consistent and was not driven by any specific event. The NAACP spent the
first fifty years of its existence testifying before Congress in an effort to gain
inclusion for blacks in civil society. The group fought for equal protection
under the law and the right to vote. When representatives of the NAACP
testified, they urged legislators to pass antilynching legislation to protect

blacks from mob violence. In the 1950s, the NAACP supported the "Powell amendments," which called for an end to discrimination by entities that received federal governmental funds. Today, the NAACP testifies on a variety of issues. Their representatives present witness testimony to ensure that blacks are receiving fair treatment in the criminal justice system, speaking out against, for example, the unfairness of mandatory sentences. NAACP representatives have also testified on the importance of eliminating discrimination in the public and private sector. Consistent with the NAACP's fight to eliminate discrimination in the lending community, in the late 2000s the NAACP testified at a mortgage discrimination lending hearing. In the 110th Congress in 2007, at the hearing *Legislative Proposals Reforming Mortgage Practices* before the House Committee on Financial Services, Hilary Shelton, director of the NAACP's Washington Bureau, addressed disparity in lending to black and white Americans: "Predatory lending is unequivocally a major civil rights issue for our times. As study after study has conclusively shown, predatory lenders consistently target African Americans, Latinos, Asians, Pacific Islanders, Native Americans, the elderly, and women at such a disproportionately high rate that the effect is devastating to not only individuals and families but to whole communities as well" (66).

The NAACP also testified at hearings that examined the portrayal of minorities in the media and discrimination at the National Institutes of Health. In the 111th Congress, it spent time testifying against racial profiling. Moreover, the group has expanded its civil rights advocacy beyond race to include protecting the rights of women. In the 95th Congress (1977–1978), for example, the NAACP testified at a hearing on a bill that would ban sex discrimination on the basis of pregnancy.

As this example suggests, while the NAACP continues to focus on civil rights issues, its representatives present testimony on an array of issues that do not fall solely under the umbrella of black civil rights, social welfare, or race relations.[6] The NAACP spends most of its time testifying in the area of government operations policy. This is the top category of House hearings testimony, representing 12 percent of the more than fifty thousand hearings held between 1951 and 2014 (see table 5.1). As defined by the Policy Agenda Project, "government operations" deals with how Congress manages the functions of the federal bureaucracy. The category includes appropriations hearings for the federal bureaucracy and oversight of the U.S. Census Bureau, U.S. Postal Service, and Internal Revenue Service.

The LCCR also does an excellent job of representing the interests of blacks. From 1951 through 2014, the group spent 54 percent of its time

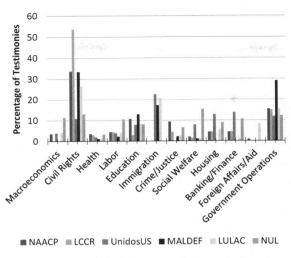

5.2. Minority Civil Rights Organizations Testimony by Issue Area, 82nd-113th Congress (1951–2014)

Table 5.1. House Hearings by Policy Area, 82nd–113th Congress (1951–2014)

Policy area	Number of hearings held	Percentage of hearings held
Government operations	5931	12%
Defense	5674	11%
International affairs	4126	8%
Banking/finance	4042	8%
Public lands	3981	8%
Health	3286	6%
Transportation	2636	5%
Law/crime	2450	5%
Environment	2391	5%
Energy	2234	4%
Science/technology	2076	4%
Agriculture	2026	4%
Macroeconomics	1540	3%
Labor	1514	3%
Education	1492	3%
Civil rights and civil liberties	**1471**	**3%**
Social welfare	1210	2%
Foreign trade	1193	2%
Housing	1093	2%
Immigration	491	1%
Totals	50,857	

testifying on civil rights issues (see figure 5.2). This advocacy included testifying at hearings to eliminate drug sentencing disparities between crack and powder cocaine, and enacting hate-crimes legislation and anti–racial profiling legislation. In the 105th Congress (1997–1998), LCCR president and chief executive officer Wade Henderson testified on the impact of disparities in drug-related sentencing legislation on blacks. He argued that Congress should reduce the disparities because blacks were disproportionately arrested and convicted for possession of crack, even though they represented a smaller proportion of users of crack than whites. Because the LCCR is a coalition of many advocacy groups, it has much broader scope than simply representing black interests. More recent LCCR testimony has involved civil rights for people with disabilities and women's rights.

The National Urban League testified only thirteen times before a House committee in the period of the 61st through 81st Congresses (1911–1950). During the civil rights era, representatives of the group began to testify in support of programs to increase the economic empowerment of blacks. From 1951 through 2014, the group spent 14.2 percent of its time testifying on social welfare issues and 12 percent on civil rights issues (see figure 5.2). This advocacy included testifying at hearings to ensure funding for food stamps and affordable housing. The organization also testifies at hearings in the macroeconomic policy dimension. They focus on efforts to increase employment opportunities for blacks in urban areas.

In a general sense, then, representatives of black civil rights organizations have presented testimony in areas of priority to black constituents, providing sustained and positive advocacy. Although criminal justice issues are not identified as top concerns in black public opinion polls, criminal justice has commanded attention from the Black Lives Matter Movement and from scholars critical of black civil rights organizations, who argue that the organizations have not done enough to advocate on this front. The next section examines the testimony efforts of black civil rights groups in this policy dimension.

Criminal Justice Advocacy: A Critique

In *The New Jim Crow: Mass Incarceration in the Age of Colorblindness*, Michelle Alexander argues that civil rights organizations such as the NAACP and the LCCR did not place the mass incarceration of blacks high on their advocacy agenda. She found that the LCCR did not include criminal justice issues on its roll-call voting scorecards, nor did the NAACP's website in 2008 significantly highlight the importance of mass incarceration as a problem for black Americans. She concedes that civil rights organizations did work in the criminal justice sphere to eliminate drug-related sentencing disparities and zero-tolerance policies, but she argues that they could have done more. According to Alexander (2010, 11), "No one visiting the [NAACP's] website would learn that the mass incarceration of African Americans had already eviscerated many of the hard-earned gains it urged its members to protect."

Yet there does not appear to be much evidence to support Alexander's contention regarding the NAACP's lack of attention to criminal justice issues. The NAACP did list criminal justice issues as a legislative priority. In 1989, and again in 1992, the NAACP passed resolutions directing the organization to devote efforts to addressing the increasing number of blacks in prison. In 1992, the NAACP introduced resolutions at its annual convention calling for the decriminalization of drugs, and in 1998 it passed a resolution titled "Eradication of Trafficking and Use of Controlled Drugs."[7] From the 109th Congress through the 111th Congress, the Washington Bureau listed criminal justice issues, such as eliminating the disparity between crack and powder cocaine and mandatory sentencing, among its legislative priorities. Thus, criminal justice was prioritized in the NAACP's policy documents and directives.

The amount of time the NAACP spent in testimony on criminal justice does lend some support to Alexander's argument, however; the NAACP and the LCCR did not prioritize action by Congress on mass incarceration through testimony. From 1951 through 2014, the NAACP and LCCR testified on criminal justice issues less frequently than they testified in other policy areas. The NAACP focused the majority of its efforts on civil rights, and only a few of the issues in this category addressed criminal justice. Figure 5.2 shows that the NAACP testified thirty-one times (9.28 of its agenda) in the criminal justice area, compared to sixteen times (33.62 percent of its agenda) on civil rights and fifty-three times (15.36 percent of its agenda) on government operations. The LCCR testified on sentencing disparities, but only in the 104th Congress (1995–1996). The LCCR devoted 4.48 percent of its agenda to testifying in this area. The NAACP and LCCR combined testified only thirty-five times in the criminal justice policy area.

Lack of testimony at hearings might be understood as a simple function of party polarization, as a Republican-controlled House was unlikely to hold hearings on these issues and thus would not invite civil rights groups to testify. The multivariate analysis shows that party polarization does have a negative affect on how frequently the NAACP testifies. Although this finding is not specific to criminal justice issues, I expect it to extend to criminal justice.

Another plausible explanation for the limited scope of civil rights group testimony on criminal justice issues—especially since Democrats controlled the House more frequently than Republicans in the period 1951 to 2014—is that leaders of civil rights organizations believed the criminal justice system did not affect all blacks, and they tried to focus on issues such as affirmative action that affected the largest number of black Americans (Cohen 1999; Strolovitch 2007).

The examination of witness testimony, along with consideration of Alexander's critique, demonstrates that black civil rights organizations are effective—if imperfect—at representing the interests of blacks through witness testimony. Blacks want these organizations to be active on civil rights and social welfare. They are certainly as successful in presenting witness testimony as they are in drawing attention to their issues through committee markups.

The next section examines whether Latino civil rights groups have met with similar success.

Responsiveness to Latino Issues

Latino civil rights organizations are effective at representing the interests of Latinos. Latinos rank education, the economy or jobs, health care, and immigration as the most salient problems facing the Latino community. Latino civil rights organizations devoted much attention to these issues.[8] According to UnidosUS's president Janet Murguia—in the 2007 hearing *Comprehensive Immigration Reform* before a subcommittee of the Judiciary Committee—"For us, immigration policy is a civil rights issue, and that is why our community engages so deeply in this policy debate" (68).

From the 90th Congress (1967–1968) through the 113th Congress (2013–2014), UnidosUS testified before House committees 102 times; MALDEF, 93 times; and LULAC, 75 times. Figure 5.2 shows that immigration hearings were the top testimony area for UnidosUS, representing 22.3 percent of its total testimony activity, and immigration was the second most important area of testimony for LULAC, at 20 percent, and third most important for MALDEF, at 17 percent. UnidosUS and MALDEF have been the leading proponents of comprehensive immigration reform at the federal level. These groups devote significant efforts to lobbying on the issue both inside and outside of Congress, and they have used their expertise to become a leading source of information for Congress. In a 2007 hearing before the House Judiciary committee in the 110th Congress, UnidosUS president Murguia stated:

> You will not be surprised to hear that immigration is a critical issue for the Latino community, though the reasons for this go well beyond what most Americans understand. The majority of Hispanic Americans are not immigrants; 60% of our community are natives of the United States. Immigration policy obviously has a deep impact on those of us who are foreign born, but it also affects the rest of us in multiple ways. It directly affects those of us with immigrant family members and those who wish to reunite with their closest family members abroad. It also has an enormous impact on public perceptions of Latinos as Americans. NCLR receives an awful lot of mail from people telling us to go back to where we came from. In my case, that would be Kansas, and I'm guessing that would come as a surprise to the people who write to me. (68)

Although LULAC's witness testimony demonstrates that LULAC was a clear advocate in the immigration area, most of the group's testimony on immigration pertained to deliberations on the Immigration Reform and Control Act of 1982 and 1983. From 1999 through 2014, LULAC testified only two times on House hearings held on illegal immigration in the 106th Congress (1999–2000). The extent to which LULAC advocates on immigration in the twenty-first century is largely unknown and cannot by determined by witness testimony or through lobbying disclosure. Thus, the largest Latino membership organization is currently silent in representing Latino immigration interests in Congress using these traditional advocacy methods.

Sustained advocacy in educational policy is another focus of Latino civil rights groups, with witness testimony on this subject ranking fourth for MALDEF at 12.9 percent and for LULAC at 8 percent, and sixth for UnidosUS at 7.84 percent. This level of attention is significant, considering that only 3 percent of congressional hearings occur in this policy area. MALDEF's attention to educational policy has been sustained over time, whereas UnidosUS's and LULAC's focus has been episodic. In the late 1970s and mid-1980s, MALDEF testified mostly to obtain access to and funding for higher education for Latinos. In the 1990s, the organization testified at hearings advocating for fair testing standards and examining the impact of the No Child Left Behind legislation on English learners. UnidosUS testified mostly at hearings reauthorizing higher education programming and in 2008 reauthorizing expiring federal elementary and secondary education programs, which Latino civil rights organizations supported. LULAC spent most of its time testifying on bilingual vocational training in the early to mid-1980s and has not testified much in the education policy area since 1997.

In addition, UnidosUS and MALDEF devote time to addressing Latino concerns about the economy and jobs. Their advocacy in this area pertains primarily to civil rights, housing, and banking and financial services. For UnidosUS, testimony in the banking and finance category ranked second, at 13.7 percent; MALDEF did not testify in this category. The largest increase in UnidosUS testimony on the economy and jobs came during the financial crisis of the late 2000s. From 2007 through 2010, representatives of the group testified approximately fourteen times—more than they had done in their previous fifty years of testifying before Congress in this specific policy area. In the 110th Congress, UnidosUS testified at hearings regarding subprime lending and how it led to high rates of home foreclosures. Most of MALDEF's testimony dedicated to improving Latino economic conditions was included in the civil rights category, representing 33 percent of the group's testimony. MALDEF testified in hearings that centered on the enforcement of equal employment laws designed to combat discrimination in employment, housing, and lending.

UnidosUS, LULAC, and MALDEF have devoted considerable time to testifying in the area of government operations policy. Most of UnidosUS's witness testimony in this dimension focused on ensuring that Latinos and blacks were accurately counted in the U.S. Census. In the 105th Congress (1997–1998), UnidosUS opposed efforts by the Census Bureau to create a multiracial category from concern that this new category would dilute census representation of the Latino community. In the 1997 hearing *Federal Measures of Race and Ethnicity and the Implications for the 2000 Census* before the Committee on Government Reform and Oversight, the UnidosUS policy analyst Eric Rodriguez articulated the group's position at the hearing: "In its current form, the addition of a multiracial category's effectiveness in any of these areas is questionable. Given that Latinos experienced at least a five percent undercount in 1990, the inclusion of such a term could mean less accurate or incomplete data in 2000. The Census must strive for questions/responses that will give us the best data, and that can be shown to improve the accuracy and specificity of the Census" (324). Despite the salience of the health-care issue to Latino voters, Latino groups do not testify much in this issue area. Over their fifty-year history, UnidosUS and MALDEF have only testified once each on health care issues: UnidosUS testified at a hearing relating to health equity for Latinos in 2007, and MALDEF testified at a hearing on health and the environment in 1981.

Although Latinos do not list race relations in their top-five policy preferences, it is in their top ten; Latinos continue to experience discrimination in employment and housing. From 1951 through 2014, as figure 5.2 shows, civil rights hearings were the top testimony area for MALDEF and LULAC, representing 33.3 percent and 25.3 percent of their total testimony activity, respectively. For UnidosUS, civil rights ranked fifth, at 10.6 percent of its total testimony. MALDEF is one of the few groups that has consistently testified on traditional civil rights issues since its inception, and groups such as LULAC and UnidosUS are called less frequently to testify in this area. From the late 1960s through 2014, MALDEF testified on hearings relating to housing discrimination, voting rights issues, and predatory lending. UnidosUS and LULAC used to testify at many of these same hearings; however, after the 103rd Congress (1993–1994), the frequency with which these groups were invited to testify in civil rights decreased. Again, this could be partly due to the decision of these groups to classify immigration as primarily a civil rights issue.

For Latino groups, then, consideration of witness testimony finds that Latino civil rights organizations are effectively representing the interests of Latinos in policy changes in the areas of immigration, education, the economy and jobs. Their testimony support for change in the health care policy dimension has been less strong.

Civil rights organizations have provided more congressional testimony since the passage of the VRA than they did prior to its passage, but we still might expect to find that rising political polarization and GOP control of Congress affects their ability to testify. In the previous chapter, I found that the presence of black legislators on House committees explained the likelihood of civil rights organizations' receiving committee markup action on bills that the organizations supported. The next section examines whether the presence of black and Latino legislators produces a similar result for the likelihood that civil rights groups will be called to testify before House committees.

Congressional Diversity and Civil Rights
Organization Testimony

To determine whether congressional diversity leads to more opportunities for civil rights organizations to testify before Congress, and thereby leads to greater legislative success for civil rights organizations, I examine witness testimony for the major black and Latino civil rights organizations. From the founding year of each civil rights organization, I examine the number of times the NAACP, NUL, UnidosUS, MALDEF, LULAC, and the LCCR testified before House committees. I look at witness testimony from the 61st through 113th Congresses (1909–2014) for the NAACP, NUL, and LULAC; the 82nd through 113th Congresses (1951–2014) for the LCCR; and the 90th through 113th Congresses (1969–2014) for UnidosUS and MALDEF. I obtained witness testimony data from ProQuest Congressional.

I measure diversity by calculating the combined percentage of black and Latino legislators in the House. The proportion of diversity increased significantly in the 1980s and 1990s as blacks and Latinos were incorporated into the electorate. I also examine several alternative explanations for how frequently civil rights groups testify in the House. The political party that has majority control of the chamber has the power to set the congressional agenda by determining how many hearings to hold and whom to invite to testify. Party control of the House is important in influencing when civil rights groups testify, especially after the passage of the VRA, when the Democratic Party became associated with supporting black and Latino civil rights and other progressive causes. The minority party has limited ability to affect the political agenda. Therefore, I test whether party control of the House affects the likelihood of civil rights groups' being invited to testify before committees.

I use political polarization to indicate the ideological differences between the average Democratic and Republican House member. I account for the impact of the president on hearings activity with a measure of divided government. The House might conduct more hearings, for example, when the presidency is controlled by a different party; in this way, hearings can be a form of oversight of the executive branch. I control for the total number of hearings held in Congress to show that opportunities for groups to testify is not simply a function of the House holding more hearings. Because witness testimony is a count, I use a Poisson regression to estimate the likelihood of civil rights groups testifying before a House committee.

Increased Witness Opportunities for Black Civil Rights Groups

I find that the presence of minority legislators in the House increases opportunities for civil rights organizations to testify before House committees. With the exception of the NUL, major civil rights organizations testify more frequently when the combined presence of black and Latino legislators in the House is greater (see table 5.2). As the proportion of black and Latino legislators increased from 1910 through 2014, the NAACP testified more frequently in the House. Figure 5.3 shows that when the proportion of black and Latino legislators was 1 percent of House membership, the NAACP testified an average of 2.5 times per congressional session. When the proportion of minority legislators was at its highest at 17.6 percent, the NAACP testified thirty-two times per session. Much of this increase in testimony can be attributed to black and Latino legislators serving on key committees to which the NAACP testified. Figure 5.4 shows that from 1951 through 2014, the NAACP testified most frequently before House Judi-

Table 5.2. Likelihood of Civil Rights Groups Testifying at House Hearings

Explanatory variables	NAACP	LCCR	UnidosUS	MALDEF
Proportion of black and Latino	15.33**	22.94*	22.22**	44.20**
members	(4.03)	(12.14)	(7.82)	(16.15)
Divided party control of House	.133	.342	.702	.666
and presidency	(.152)	(.312)	(.466)	(.456)
GOP control of House	−.684**	−1.26	−2.02**	−.799
	(.232)	(.568)	(.583)	(.615)
Total number of House hearings	.000**	.001⁺	.000	.001*
held	(.000)	(.000)	(.000)	(.000)
Polarization	−3.91**	−3.09	−.547	−10.60**
	(.000)	(3.07)	(1.28)	(3.28)
Constant	2.59**	−.412	−1.12	2.16**
	(.623)	(1.55)	(.934)	(1.18)
Log pseudo-likelihood	−140.16	−59.74	−45.32	−59.09
Wald chi-square	96.11	27.39	193.40	19.77
Pseudo-R^2	.000	.249	.378	.330
N	53	32	23	23

Note: Witness testimony covers: 61st to 113th Congress (1909–2014) for the NAACP, 82nd to 113th Congress (1951–2014) for the LCCR; and the 90th to 113th Congress (1969–2014) for UnidosUS and MALDEF. Robust standard errors are in parentheses.
*$p < .05$ (two-tailed). **$p < .01$ (two-tailed). ⁺$p < .10$ (two-tailed).

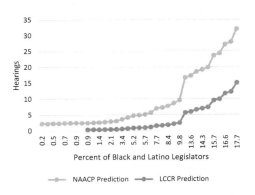

5.3. Black Interest Group Testimony in the House (1951–2014)

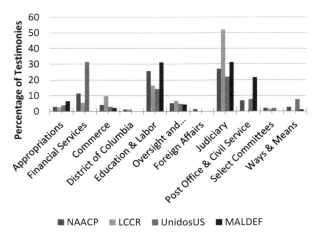

5.4. Minority Civil Rights Organizations Testimony by Committee (1951–2014)

ciary, Education and Workforce, and Financial Services Committees. These committees were the most diverse in the House, partly because minority legislators selected onto them. The importance of this diversity is not lost on Hilary Shelton, head of the NAACP's Washington Bureau: "These are committees that have great influence on the concerns of the African American community. Committees like the Judiciary, which could touch on hate crimes, civil rights enforcement and voting rights enforcement. We couldn't ask for a chair that better represents the challenges in the Judiciary Committee and civil rights than John Conyers."[9]

In the early years of the NAACP's existence, from the 61st through 75th Congresses (1909–1938), no black members served in the House and only eleven Latinos served. The NAACP testified an average of 0.66 times per congressional term in this period. Although the results show that both the increase in hearings held over time and Democratic control of the House are significant variables—that is, that both greater numbers of hearings being held and Democratic control make it more likely that civil rights organizations will testify—the increase of minority legislators in the House nonetheless remains a significant variable in explaining the enhanced testimony opportunities for civil rights groups. Neither divided party control of the House nor the political party of the presidency affects how frequently civil rights groups testify.

House diversity similarly plays a significant role in increasing the opportunities for the LCCR to testify before House committees. When the proportion of minority legislators is at the maximum of 17.6 percent, the group testifies approximately 14.9 times per Congress. The predicted rate of testimony of 1.6 times per congressional term is much lower when the proportion of minority legislators is close to the mean House minority membership of 8 percent.

The conservative ideological shift in the House and increasing polarization associated with GOP control of the chamber are the prominent factors affecting the witness testimony of civil rights organizations. From the 104th Congress (1995–1996) through the 113th Congress (2013–2014), the Republican Party controlled the House during eight of the ten Congresses. GOP control of the chamber is directly and negatively associated with group testimony for the NAACP and the LCCR. The NAACP testified 2.9 times per congressional term under GOP control, compared to 5.8 times per term under Democratic control. The same applies to UnidosUS, whose representatives testified 0.93 times per session in the Republican-controlled House, compared to 7 times under the Democrats.

Although diversity has increased the likelihood of civil rights groups testifying before Congress overall, this likelihood varies considerably depending on which party controls the chamber. In the 2010s, the average amount of testimony by minority interest groups was lower than it had been when Southern segregationists had significant power in the Democratic Party. The second-lowest point of NAACP testimony before the House occurred between 2011 and 2014 (the 112th and 113th Congresses). The average of 1.5 for this period was lower than the average of 6.2 in 1951–1960, when Southern Democrats were actively working to keep civil rights off the congressional agenda. This is because the ability of the NAACP to provide testimony has been significantly affected by GOP control of Congress and by party polarization. The NAACP is not called to testify, or perhaps does not want to testify, in periods when the GOP is unlikely to promote its agenda. Average witness testimony by the NAACP has declined since 1991, but it never sank below its average for the pre–civil rights era until the 112th and 114th Congresses (2011–2016).

Despite GOP control and the increased workload of the House since the 1950s, civil rights groups testified at higher rates than they did before the passage of the VRA. When Democrats are in control, civil rights groups representing black interests receive more opportunities to testify. Conversely, when Republicans control the House, their opportunities to testify diminish to levels that are below the pre-VRA years. Thus, party control of the Congress, in combination with diversity, plays a key role in the future advocacy efforts of civil rights organizations.

Increased Witness Opportunities for Latino Civil Rights Groups

The presence of minority legislators in the House increases witness testimony opportunities for UnidosUS and MALDEF, but not for LULAC (see table 5.2). Looking first at UnidosUS, when the proportion of minority legislators is at its height of 17.6 percent, then the group testifies 16.6 times per Congress. Conversely, figure 5.5 shows that UnidosUS testifies only 3 times when the proportion of minority legislators is close to the chamber average of 12 percent. Figure 5.4 shows that from 1951 through 2014, UnidosUS testified the most before House Judiciary, Education and Workforce, and Financial Services—the most diverse committees in the House, as well as the committees that cover issues of greatest importance to the Latino community.

Diversity also plays a significant role in increasing the opportunities for MALDEF to testify before House committees. When the proportion of minority legislators is at the maximum of 17.6 percent, MALDEF testifies approximately 60.4 times per Congress. The predicted rate of testimony is much lower, at 1.8 times, when the proportion of minority legislators is close to the average minority membership of 10 percent.

House polarization does limit testimony opportunities for Latino civil rights organizations. Table 5.2 shows that party polarization and GOP con-

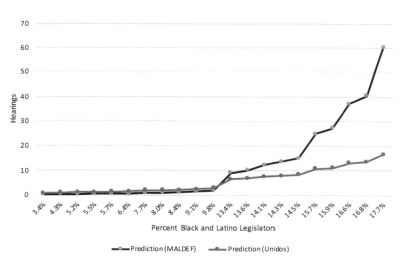

Percent Black and Latino Legislators

━━ Prediction (MALDEF)   ━━ Prediction (Unidos)

5.5. Latino Interest Group Testimony in the House (1951–2014)

trol of the chamber are directly and negatively associated with group testimony for UnidosUS and MALDEF.

On the whole, then, analysis of civil rights organizations' testimony shows that increased minority presence in the House improves these minority organizations' opportunities to testify—Republican control of the House significantly and consistently moderates these opportunities. Because of civil rights organizations' reliance on legislative advocates, however, we should also expect that the increase in the number of members in the Congressional Black Caucus and Congressional Hispanic Caucus in the 1990s would have expanded the capacity of these organizations to advocate for minority interests through testimony. The efforts by members of Congress to support minority interests and the degree to which they subsidize and complement the advocacy efforts of civil rights organizations—or both—are the subjects of the next sections.

Legislative Advocates and Committee Testimony

The investment of civil rights groups in redistricting litigation led to long-term benefits for their members: the creation of majority-minority districts made it more likely black and Latino candidates would be elected to the House and thereby increased the strength of the CBC and CHC. As a result of the greater organizational capacity of the CBC and CHC, civil rights organizations no longer have to depend only on their own efforts or those of one or two legislative champions, as they did with Adam Clayton Powell Jr. or Edward Roybal.

From 1930 to 1964, black legislators testified a total of sixty-six times before congressional committees, compared to eighty-two for the NAACP.[10] Since black legislators organized and their numbers have increased, however, black legislators testify on average more frequently than do representatives of the top-three civil rights organizations combined. This is significant, because civil rights organizations rely on legislative advocates appearing before congressional committees to champion their policy interests. From 1970 through 2016, members of the CBC testified more frequently in absolute terms and on average than did representatives of civil rights organizations across all policy dimensions with the exception of civil rights. The CBC and CHC, although not formally recognized as interest groups, are two of the most powerful advocacy organizations for racial and ethnic minorities. Their member legislators speak about the provisions of bills and how bills will impact their district, state, or the country.

Black Legislators' Witness Testimony

Today, black members of Congress have a significant presence in the House and testify at hearings. These members can work with the NAACP and other groups. Unlike civil rights groups, neither the CBC nor CHC are required to register to lobby. Even if the caucuses did have to register, testifying before congressional committees is not considered lobbying under federal law. Unlike civil rights organizations, black legislators also testify in areas that are not explicitly race related but are considered important to black interests, such as education and employment. Indeed, civil rights might be a salient area for black voters, but it is not the area in which black legislators testify most frequently. Congress spends most of its time holding hearings on government operations, and correspondingly, black legislators spend most of their time testifying in this area. Figure 5.6 shows that from 1971 through 2016, black legislators distributed their testimony at hearings in the following policy dimensions: 19 percent in government operations, 9 percent in transportation, 6 percent in public lands, 6 percent in macroeconomics, and 6 percent in foreign affairs. The highest proportion of House hearings, at 12 percent of hearings held, fell under the government operations category, which includes hearings related to appropriations for federal agencies, nominations of federal officials, and the operation of the U.S. Postal Service. Although most hearings in the government operations category do not pertain to explicitly racial issues, many issues testified on by black legislators do address black interests, as such subjects as acquiring funding for educational and job-training programs are classified in this category rather than the education and labor policy dimension.

Figures 5.6 and 5.7 show that as black legislators' numbers increased, so did their testimony at appropriations hearings. In the 100th Congress (1987–1988), black legislators testified only eight times at appropriations hearings on government operations policy; however, in the 103rd Congress (1993–1994), they testified nineteen times at appropriations hearings.

Black legislators also provide significant advocacy benefits to minority civil rights organizations in support of black higher educational institutions. Black legislators and the NAACP frequently list acquiring funding for historically black colleges and universities (HBCUs) and job training as legislative priorities. Specifically, the NAACP listed funding for HBCUs as a legislative priority from the 109th Congress (2005–2006) to the 113th Congress (2013–2014), but the group did not testify at appropriations hearings at which funding for these universities was discussed. The NAACP testified only two times during this period on government operations pol-

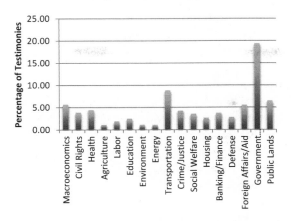

5.6. Black Legislators' House Testimony by Issue Area, 92nd–114th Congress (1971–2016)

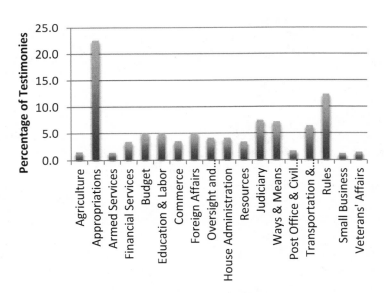

5.7. Black Legislators' House Testimony by Committee, 92nd–114th Congress (1971–2016)

icy, with none of this testimony pertaining to appropriations. Instead, it testified on preparing election officials for the 2016 elections and clean energy legislation.

The NAACP relies on black legislators to testify and advocate for funding for HBCUs in the appropriations arena. Black legislators testify at the appropriations hearings for the Departments of Labor, Health and Human

Services, and Education to advocate for HBCU funding. In 1997 in the 105th Congress, Rep. William Clay (D-MO) testified in favor of funding for HBCUs before the House Appropriations subcommittee:

> The primary source of institutional support for these institutions is Title III of the Higher Education Act which has been frozen for the past three years. It is critical that additional and adequate funding is made available for both undergraduate and graduate institutional support. In addition, if HBCUs are to continue their impressive record of producing a disproportionate number of Black college graduates, additional support for their graduates to pursue a graduate education is necessary. For Black colleges to maintain their strong faculties, it is imperative that they are provided more funding to enable them to prepare their graduates for doctoral studies—particularly in the areas of science and technology. (1995)

Black legislators are not the only members who support HBCUs, but they are the main members who show up to testify for HBCUs.

Civil Rights Advocacy

Black legislators also play an important role in civil rights advocacy. Although only 3 percent of House hearings are devoted to civil rights and civil liberties, black legislators devote 5 percent of their time to testifying in this area. This is lower than the NAACP and LCCR in terms of proportion; however, the overall number is closer, with black legislators testifying 72 times from 1976 through 2014, compared to the NAACP's representatives testifying 116 times. Thus, black legislators compete favorably in providing substantive representation of black and other minorities in this policy area.

Many of the civil rights issues testified on by black legislators were related to the policy priorities testified on by the NAACP. In general, civil rights groups are thought to provide a subsidy to legislators (Hall and Deardorff 2006), but clearly legislators can also subsidize the efforts of minority advocacy groups, especially when they testify in the same policy area. For example, there were eighty-two civil rights hearings held in the 110th Congress. CBC members testified at six House hearings, and the NAACP also testified at six. In all the cases, the issues addressed in this testimony were similar, or the positions taken by the CBC and NAACP were similar. CBC members testify more frequently than do representatives of the NAACP and the LCCR. The CBC, NAACP, and LCCR are fairly equal in the amount of testimony they devote to civil rights issues, but members of the CBC testify in other areas related to minority interests that are not addressed by the NAACP or LCCR. Although they take similar positions, on civil rights these groups do not always testify at the same hearing. This provides for more coverage and advocacy on these issues. For instance, in the 110th Congress (2007–2008), black legislators testified at a hearing to support a bill that would eliminate health-care disparities, but the NAACP did not. Although the NAACP did not testify, black legislators effectively represented the policy interests of the NAACP at the hearing.

Particularly in a context where polarization limits opportunities for civil rights groups to testify in a Republican-controlled House, it becomes important for CBC members in Congress to provide a voice for the concerns of civil rights organizations. However, the average rate of CBC testimony has itself declined as a result of congressional polarization. The GOP has become far more conservative, as evident in the infusion into Congress of Tea Party activists after the 2010 election, when Republicans regained control of the House from Democrats. Across the board in all policy dimensions, the CBC and CHC have declined in their rate of testimony before House committees.

Criminal Justice Advocacy

Civil rights organizations have fought for equal treatment of blacks by the criminal justice system. As we have seen, since the NAACP's founding, the organization led efforts to get antilynching legislation enacted (Francis 2014). In the 2000s, however, the NAACP is no longer the primary civil rights organization advocating for the fair treatment of blacks and other minorities. Many other groups have developed and provide advocacy in this area, with the CBC becoming one of the strongest advocates on criminal justice. We saw in chapter 1's discussion of the Fair Sentencing Act that the fight to address the impact of the sale and use of illicit drugs such as cocaine in black communities was a major focus of black legislators. In the 1980s, when groups such as the NAACP and the LCCR, as well as the Sentencing Commission, reported and testified at congressional hearings that these tougher laws disproportionately targeted and sentenced blacks and Latinos to prison, Rep. Rangel (D-NY), who had once championed such tougher laws, switched his position, opposed the tougher laws as a solution.

In fact, black legislators have spent more time than civil rights organizations testifying in the criminal justice policy area, with the specific aim of eliminating unfair and mandatory sentences resulting from drug sentencing legislation. From 1951 through 2014, when the NAACP testified thirty-one times on criminal justice, black legislators presented testimony on seventy-eight separate occasions. Rep. Charles Rangel introduced a bill in every session between 1993 and 2009 calling for a reduction in sentencing disparities. In that same period, several GOP members introduced bills to increase penalties for use and sale of powder cocaine to match the strict sentences given to people convicted of using and selling crack. Later, other Democrats started introducing their version of the sentence-reduction bill, including Rep. Maxine Waters (D-CA) and Rep. Bobby Scott (D-VA). In the 111th Congress (2009–2010), when the sentencing disparities legislation was passed, Senate bill 1789 was sponsored by Sen. Dick Durbin (D-IL). Hearings were held in 1986 regarding the growing problem of crack and powder cocaine. In the 99th Congress, the House Select Committee on Narcotics Abuse and Control, chaired by Rep. Rangel, and the Select Committee on Children, Youth, and Families both held hearings.

From the earlier discussion, it is clear, however, that minority-group testimony in criminal justice also declined because black legislators were sharing the load of advocating in this policy area where the NAACP used to be the primary champion. Despite the efforts by black legislators to seek fair treatment, critics argued that they were not doing enough to solve the problems. Just as Alexander criticized the NAACP and LCCR on this point, she also argued that the Congressional Black Caucus did not prioritize criminal justice issues. Criminal justice was not mentioned, for example, in a letter that the CBC sent to community leaders requesting that they identify policy priorities, such as housing, immigration, and taxes. Alexander (2010, 10) writes: "No mention was made of criminal justice. 'Re-entry' as listed, but a community leader who was interested in criminal justice reform had to check the box labeled 'other.'"

Black Legislators and International Issues

Although never ranked highly by blacks as a policy priority in public-opinion polls, civil rights organizations have an expressed commitment to represent the interests of blacks living in the United States and in other countries. Despite this stated purpose, black nationalists such as Malcolm X and Kwame Ture (formerly Stokely Carmichael), as well as some scholars, have argued that in the 1950s and 1960s civil rights organizations such as the NAACP and Southern Christian Leadership Conference failed to link the black civil rights movement to the broader push for human rights

(Anderson 2003; Ture and Hamilton 1967). Even though the NAACP has paid attention to international issues in its convention resolutions and legislative priorities, such as opposing apartheid and supporting sanctions against the South African government in the 1980s, international issues are not the main province of these groups. I find that black legislators help civil rights groups the most with advocacy for international issues relating to the black diaspora. In the 1970s, Rep. Parren Mitchell advocated for the United States to divest from South Africa and to impose economic sanctions. The CBC was instrumental in founding TransAfrica, one of the leading advocacy groups calling for sanctions on South Africa (Tillery 2011). Consistent pressure from advocacy groups and legislative advocates such as Rep. Ron Dellums (D-CA) pressured the Reagan administration to enact tougher sanctions. These sanctions, joined by others from the international community, helped lead to the demise of the apartheid regime in South Africa. In this action, civil rights groups relied on black legislators to press their case before Congress.

In the twenty-first century, that commitment to addressing international interests has not changed. In the 2000s, black legislators selected on committees with jurisdiction over international issues. In the 111th Congress (2009–2010), black legislators accounted for 15 percent of the House Foreign Affairs committee. Their membership on this committee ranked third among all committees, with only Homeland Security and Judiciary committees ranked higher. As a result, black legislators testified 101 times before House committees focusing on foreign affairs. The NAACP, by comparison, testified only three times in this policy dimension, and the NUL and LCCR did not testify at all. The greater number of black legislators in House increased the capacity of blacks to advocate in areas beyond the traditional civil rights agenda, providing advocacy in foreign affairs. Considering that blacks in the United States are not primarily immigrants from the Caribbean and African continent, this advocacy fulfills a commitment to representing the interests of all blacks.

Overall, then, black civil rights organizations' legislative advocates provide crucial support in the area of testimony. This support is primary, with black committee members forming relationships with specific organizations and inviting their representatives to testify; it is also supplementary, with black legislators testifying in support of the same issues and bills on which civil rights organizations testify; and it is complementary, in the sense that black legislators step forward to testify on issues that civil rights organizations are not invited to represent or to advocate for civil rights groups' legislative agenda in the context of a polarized,

Republican-controlled house in which civil rights group testimony is not welcome. This picture suggests that civil rights groups' strategy of increasing minority representation and cultivating legislative advocates has been highly successful—although it is important to note that in the Republican-controlled Congress, black representatives' opportunities to testify also markedly decline, suggesting limitations to the strategy that civil rights organizations might need to overcome.

Latino Legislators' Witness Testimony

Latinos are one of the fastest-growing demographic groups in the United States. As we have seen, the economy and education are top priorities of the Latino community. Immigration has also become a higher priority, in part because of the advocacy efforts of Latino civil rights organizations. Latino members of Congress testify more than does UnidosUS on civil rights issues, education, social welfare, criminal justice, and banking and financial issues. UnidosUS testified three times in the House during the 103rd Congress (1993–1994), for example, but Latino legislators testified 103 times in this same Congress.

Latino legislators and the Congressional Hispanic Caucus have identified immigration reform as their top priority. On this issue, witness testimony by Latino legislators matches the efforts of civil rights advocacy groups. From 1968 through 2014, Latino legislators testified thirty-four times, compared to twenty-three counts of testimony by representatives of UnidosUS and sixteen for MALDEF. Moreover, the amount of time that Latino legislators testified might understate how much effort the CHC devotes to immigration. Individual Latino members reflect the policy positions of the CHC on immigration issues even though they do not say during witness testimony that they represent the CHC.

Immigration does not rank in the top five areas in which Latino legislators testify, however. Instead, Latino legislators devote much of their efforts to testifying in areas that do not relate directly to ethnicity: government operations (16 percent, or 165 testimonies), public lands (15 percent, or 152 testimonies), transportation (9 percent, or 92 testimonies), defense (7 percent, or 70 testimonies), and macroeconomics (4 percent, or 43 testimonies). The focus on government operations is not out of step with Latino interests: public opinion surveys rate education as a top policy priority for the Latino community (figure 5.8). Latino legislators represent minority perspectives in the budgeting process and argue for greater attention to funding for Latino issues. Most of the testimony in appropriations hear-

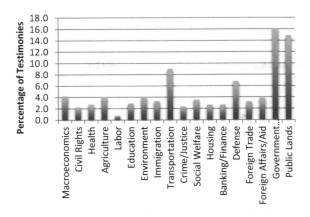

5.8. Latino Legislators' House Testimony by Issue Area, 95th–114th Congress (1977–2016)

ings before the Departments of Labor, Education, and Health and of Human Services pertain to acquiring funding for Latino-serving institutions and supporting the Job Corps program. UnidosUS and MALDEF identify education in their lobbying disclosure reports as a priority, but they are not invited to testify on these issues. Instead, UnidosUS relies on Latino legislators to testify and advocate for funding.

Latino legislators are not the only members who support Latino-serving institutions of higher learning, but they are the primary members who show up to testify in support of these institutions. In the 105th Congress, Latino legislators appealed for funding for Latino-serving institutions of higher education. In 1997 in a hearing before the House Appropriations Committee, which funds the Departments of Labor, Health and Human Services, and Education, Rep. Rubén Hinojosa (D-TX) testified in support of more funding for Hispanic-serving institutions of higher education:

As you know Hispanic-Serving Institutions (HSIs) are institutions of higher education where the Hispanic enrollment is at least 25 percent of the total student enrollment. Historically, these schools have played a pivotal role in the education of Hispanics. This is evidenced by the enrollment of 60% of the Hispanic college students in America in some 160 HSIs. HSIs have a proven record of enrolling Hispanics and compromise a solid base for launching federal support for graduate and professional opportunities. Unfortunately, these institutions have limited funds to support their growing student bodies. For this reason, we ask that the Committee consider increasing finding of $50 million for HSIs. (2100)

The volume of testimony by Latino legislators at appropriations hearings also increased as they improved their congressional representation (figure 5.9). In the 96th Congress (1979–1980), Latino legislators testified only two times at appropriations hearings in the government operations policy area. In the 103rd Congress (1993–1994), however, when Latino representation had increased from 1.5 percent to 3.8 percent of the chamber, they testified eleven times at appropriations hearings. Latinos testify primarily at the appropriations hearings for the Departments of Labor, Health and Human Services, and Education, as well as for appropriations to fund the Departments of Commerce, Justice, and State. While the education category captures some of Latino legislators' advocacy on education issues, government operations also captures advocacy in the education area as groups seek to obtain funding for educational programs.

Latino legislators do not devote as much time as do Latino interest groups to civil rights issues—at least as these issues are traditionally defined.[11] Although 3 percent of House hearings are devoted to civil rights and civil liberties, Latino legislators devote about 2 percent of their time to testifying on civil rights, ranking seventh on their list. Conversely, testimony on civil rights comprises 33 percent of MALDEF's testimony, 25 percent of LULAC's, and 10 percent of UnidosUS's. The overall num-

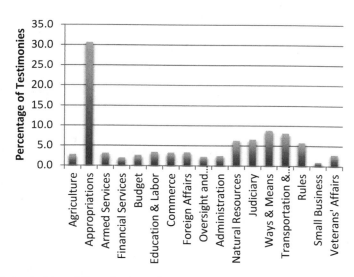

5.9. Latino Legislators' House Testimony by Committee, 95th–114th Congress (1977–2016)

ber of instances of testimony is similar, however, with Latino legislators testifying twenty-three times from the 95th through the 113th Congresses (1977–2014) compared to thirty-one times for MALDEF, nineteen times for LULAC, and eleven times for UnidosUS. The average rate of testimony on civil rights for Latino legislators is 1.21 instances per congressional term versus 1.63 for MALDEF, 1.00 for LULAC, and 0.57 for UnidosUS. If immigration is included in the broad category of civil rights, however, then Latino legislators compete favorably with civil rights organizations in providing substantive representation of Latinos in this policy area, demonstrating that Latino legislators subsidize Latino civil rights organizations. With an expanded civil rights category that includes immigration, Latino legislators testified fifty-seven times, compared to forty-seven times for MALDEF and thirty-four times each for LULAC and UnidosUS.

We find again, then, that whereas civil rights groups are generally thought to provide a subsidy to legislators, legislators can also subsidize the efforts of minority advocacy groups, especially when they testify in the same policy area.

Health Care and Latinos

In 2010, Latinos had one of the highest uninsured rates in the United States, with 33 percent of Latinos lacking health insurance coverage, compared to 20 percent of blacks and 13 percent of whites.[12] Surveys that same year indicated that health care was the top concern in the Latino community. Latino civil rights organizations expressed an interest in addressing this issue, but these organizations did not testify much at hearings related to health care from 1968 to 2014. Instead, Latino legislators testified twenty-eight times on health-care policy, compared to only two times for UnidosUS and one time for MALDEF and LULAC. In the 110th Congress and the 111th Congress, Rep. Hilda Solis (D-CA) introduced bills designed to eliminate disparities in health insurance coverage between minorities and whites. In the 2008 hearing *Addressing Disparities in Health and Healthcare*, Rep. Solis testified before the House Ways and Means Committee, on the importance of one of these bills to the Latino community: "Cultural and linguistic barriers contribute to reduced quality of care, adverse healthcare outcomes and increased racial and ethnic disparities. Just as an example, limited English proficient individuals are less likely to understand their medication instructions, less likely to use primary and preventive care, and more likely to seek care in an emergency room" (17). Smaller Latino interest groups also testified on the bill, making it unnecessary for representatives of UnidosUS and MALDEF to testify. This freed up resources to allow the major Latino civil rights groups to focus on other issues, such as civil rights pertaining to voting and legal issues related to citizenship.

As with black civil rights organizations, then, Latino interest groups show similar patterns of congressional testimony, and their relationship to minority legislators in regard to testimony is likewise both primary (increasing opportunities for groups to testify), supplementary (multiplying testimony in favor of civil rights groups' favored policy), and complementary (testifying on issues for which civil rights groups have not been invited to appear). Just as the relationship between black civil rights organizations and legislators is affected by Republican control of Congress and party polarization, so too do both Latino civil rights groups and Latino legislative advocates lose opportunities to testify in this context, which creates a challenge for advancing Latino civil rights groups' agenda.

Conclusion

The decision by a committee to hold a hearing gives organized interests an opportunity to advocate for their members while drawing greater attention to their issues. As a result of greater diversity in the House, minority civil rights organizations testify more frequently at hearings. Similar to their lobbying activity, black groups testify in the civil rights area, while Latino civil rights groups have directed their primary focus to immigration. Black groups put a lower priority on criminal justice issues, and Latino groups on racial discrimination issues, than they do on their primary agenda items, but in areas where civil rights organizations fall short in testimony because of lack of resources or access, black and Latino legislative advocates step up. Minority legislators provide a vital voice on issues that these groups support and on which they are not often called to testify. Black legislators devote much effort to testifying on criminal justice issues, and Latino legislators do the same on traditional civil rights issues.

I find, then, that testimony before congressional committees provides a robust measure of the success of civil rights organizations, showing that as Congress becomes more diverse, these organizations are more successful in advancing their legislative agenda, both through their own representatives' testimony before committees and through the testimony of their legislative allies. This positive impact of diversity for black and Latino civil rights advocacy has been counterbalanced, however, by the rise in party polarization, seen chiefly in periods of Republican control of the House. Although diversity on committees increases witness testimony opportunities for civil rights organizations, House polarization decreases the likelihood of testimony for these groups, especially when Republicans control the House. This result points to a limitation of civil rights groups' strategy for legislative success, at least in the testimony dimension. Markup results, considered in chapter 4, are fairly consistent across the various policy dimensions of interest to civil rights groups: greater diversity in Congress improves the markup success of these organizations' bills across all dimensions. Testimony, in contrast, shows more mixed outcomes. This is the case in part because the CBC and CHC have taken a complementary role, pushing forward the agenda of civil rights groups in areas where the groups cannot testify and permitting them to concentrate their resources for testimony in core areas of focus. But it also seems to be the case that the availability of opportunities to testify is more sensitive to changes in congressional control, and perhaps a more vulnerable strategy for the exercise of civil rights organizations' influence.

SIX

Conclusion

Implications for Civil Rights Advocacy in the Era of Hashtag Movements

Civil rights organizations have engaged in both insider and outsider advocacy efforts to make Congress more responsive to the policy preferences of blacks and Latinos. The passage of the Civil Rights Act of 1964 and the Voting Rights Act of 1965 removed barriers such as literacy tests, grandfather clauses, and all-white primaries that had prevented blacks from participating in formal politics (McAdam 1982; Morris 1984). In 1975, amendments to the VRA eliminated language barriers that prevented Latinos and other language minorities from voting (Garcia Bedolla 2009; Pinderhughes 1995). Despite these and other political gains made by black and Latino civil rights organizations, however, many scholars and observers have argued that political incorporation and reliance on legislative allies has compromised the ability of these groups to achieve substantial additional progress. They point to the lack of congressional action to resolve issues, such as the rise in mass incarceration of minorities, racial profiling, poverty, and the detention and deportation of Latino immigrants, as evidence that participation in formal politics has limitations in addressing minorities concerns.

According to these scholars, civil rights groups and their congressional allies have not done enough to solve these problems, and the leaders of minority civil right groups have been reluctant to represent the concerns of minorities on important issues, including criminal justice reform and the fight against HIV/AIDS in the minority community, for fear that attention to these issues will only further marginalize the people they represent (Alexander 2010; Cohen 1999; Frymer 1999; Guinier 1994; Smith 1996; Strolovitch 2007; Tate 2014). Moreover, scholars suggest that civil rights organization leaders' need to obtain resources to ensure the survival of their organizations has stymied their efforts to take on progressive battles that do not appeal to private foundation and corporate donors (Marquez 2003; Piven and Cloward 1977).

Not only are civil rights organizations charged with failure to represent the interests of all group members; their efforts to diversify Congress to make it more responsive to minority interests have been deemed misguided. In *Tyranny of the Majority*, law professor Lani Guinier (1994) argued that civil rights activists' strategy of improving advocacy by increasing the number of blacks who serve in elected office is doomed to fail. Civil rights groups were wrong to believe black legislators would have the power to help further the civil rights advocacy agenda, Guinier argues, because these legislators, as token representatives, have little power to influence their white colleagues and consequently affect the legislative agenda. Some empirical scholars have provided support for Guinier's thesis, finding that minority legislators have not necessarily improved the substantive representation of minority interests (Cameron, Epstein, and O'Halloran 1996; Hero and Tolbert 1995; Swain 1995). Furthermore, because black representatives are primarily affiliated with the Democratic Party, Republican Party control of Congress hurts the ability of blacks to get their policy preferences represented (Lublin 1997; Swain 1993). Even when Democrats control the Congress, majority status does not necessarily ensure that civil rights groups will be successful. In 2009–2010, Democrats controlled all branches of Congress and the presidency, yet they failed to pass comprehensive immigration reform, an anti–racial profiling bill, or a comprehensive jobs bill that would address high unemployment in black and Latino communities.

This book has addressed many of the concerns raised by legal scholars such as Guinier and Alexander and political scientists such as Cohen, Marquez, Strolovitch, investigating questions such as whether civil rights organizations are effective in representing black and Latino interests and whether their legislative priorities and advocacy efforts address what blacks and Latinos believe are the most important problems facing their communities. This book is one of the first studies to systematically and comprehensively examine the contents of the advocacy agenda of major black and Latino civil rights organizations, considering not just the issues included in civil rights organizations' voting scorecards but also those they report lobbying on before the federal government and how often they testify about these issues before congressional committees.

Additionally, this study has examined whether civil rights organizations' effort to help diversify the racial and ethnic composition of the House has led to more responsiveness in Congress to issues supported by these organizations. The data and analysis presented in these chapters demonstrate that the presence of more black and Latino representatives in Congress has definitively led to more opportunities for civil rights groups to testify at congressional hearings and receive more attention in the form of markup hearings on the bills lobbied on by these groups. This study goes beyond assessing whether legislators are voting the right way on issues favored by civil rights organizations to examining whether the presence of legislative advocates itself benefits civil rights groups across their entire advocacy agenda.

Although diversity in Congress has clearly benefited civil rights groups, their strategy of supporting the creation of legislative advocates has limitations for the representation of minority interests. In this final chapter, I begin with an overview of this study's findings about the effectiveness of civil rights organizations. Next, I look at how black and Latino legislators are limited by concerns of the party in how much they can push for radical policy. Additionally, I explore whether using the Voting Rights Act remains a viable vehicle for increasing diversity in the House; examine the effect that reliance on corporate or foundation funding has on the advocacy efforts of civil rights organizations; and offer some thoughts on whether hashtag movements on social media are reasonable alternatives for bringing about policy change for minorities.

Are Civil Rights Groups Effective Representatives of Black and Latino Interests?

Since the rise of the Black Lives Matter movement and immigration protests in 2006, black and Latino civil rights organizations have been criticized for not being in touch with the needs and interests of minorities—particularly those of the younger generation. The concern is that these groups have been incorporated in the political process and are no longer forceful advocates for the kind of progressive change desired by more liberal black and Latino citizens.

From my data, I find this criticism to be overstated. Groups such as UnidosUS and MALDEF have advocated consistently for the civil rights of blacks and Latinos since the 1960s, and the NAACP, NUL, and LULAC have done so for even longer. Although these groups focus mainly on civil rights for blacks and Latinos, they have expansive policy agendas that touch on a variety of policy areas, including social welfare policy, funding for black- and Latino-serving institutions of higher education, criminal justice, and immigration reform. There is some reason to be concerned, however, that the extensive attention given to immigration by Latino civil rights groups might crowd out other issues of importance to the Latino community. For blacks, civil rights organizations' focus on voting rights and criminal justice issues might detract from attention to macroeconomic policies that could benefit the African American community. Although minority interest groups are no less radical in terms of their support for civil rights issues than they were in the past, they may be reluctant to engage in policy debates that affect structural economic conditions in ways that could benefit the black community. The next sections consider these points in more detail.

Civil Rights Organizations' Representation of Black Interests

Ironically, civil rights organizations are criticized the most by mainstream media, grassroots activists, citizens, and scholars for being ineffective at advocating for minority civil rights. The NAACP, for example, was called out for its inaction in responding to police shootings of black men. Yet advocacy on criminal justice issues has always played a central role in the NAACP's agenda, and that focus has not diminished in recent years. As we have seen, the NAACP, in coalition with other civil rights groups, fought to reduce the sentencing disparity between crack and powder cocaine charges. The organization's lobbying record for the 110th and 111th Congresses shows that the NAACP spent significant time lobbying the federal government to eliminate police brutality and racial profiling. These issues are important to the black community, and civil rights organizations devote time lobbying and testifying at hearings on them.

Although scholars argue that the NAACP does not pay sufficient attention to intersectional issues, moreover, the group has expanded its advocacy to support bills that would outlaw discrimination based on sexual orientation. Although it is true that the NAACP does not make intersectional policy a core part of its agenda, it is important to remember that the NAACP is a political organization whose leaders cannot afford to isolate or divide their membership. Yet they also cannot afford to ignore issues that have a significant impact on the minority community such as the spread of HIV/AIDS or sexual assault—and they do not. The LCCR has similarly expanded the issues on which it focuses. The organization is a broad coalition of civil rights organizations but has centered much of its activity on eliminating racial and ethnic discrimination in employment, housing, and lending.

Of course, even if civil rights organizations successfully set a progressive agenda, by the time a bill gets to the floor for a vote, the impact of race or ethnicity or gender gives way to party. Black legislators must convince fellow party members that their colleagues should support a given bill. Evidence has challenged this perspective, but Guinier is right to be concerned with regard to citizen participation. Civil rights groups worry about linking so much of their agenda to legislators that they become ineffective in challenging the status quo. All politicians and interest group leaders must take this balancing act into consideration.

When Democrats controlled Congress, civil rights groups saw bills that they had lobbied on receive committee attention, especially from committees that were more racially and ethnically diverse. In the 110th and 111th Congresses, the NAACP spent most of its time advocating for more funding for job-training programs and historically black and colleges and universities, but these projects did not address the more fundamental need to lessen employment, housing, and health disparities between blacks and whites. The same is true for Latinos: immigration reform is the top-listed priority of Latino civil rights organizations, but most Latinos are not immigrants and are affected by structural issues that advocacy groups do not devote much effort to addressing.

Although civil rights issues are important to blacks, they are not considered by black citizens to be the most important public policy issues facing the black community. Education is listed as a priority for the NAACP and NUL, but it does not receive much of the group's resources in terms of lobbying or witness testimony. While black legislative advocates associated with the CBC provide witness testimony on HBCU funding, representatives of the NAACP, NUL, and LCCR have been largely silent in testimony and lobbying for higher education. Likewise, black and Latino civil rights organizations have provided limited advocacy on health care, though black and Latino citizens rank it as a high priority in polling.

Black civil rights organizations focus on civil rights, which is their niche. These groups rely on black legislators, especially those in the CBC, to push other aspects of their agenda forward. The CBC delivers with an expansive approach to representing black interests. It forwards a broad policy agenda, including civil rights, but it also advocates for access to affordable health care, job creation, and an improved economy. These legislators have resources to provide consistent advocacy in areas not covered by civil rights groups. These findings contradict critics of racial redistricting who have argued that black legislators would be marginalized by their white colleagues (Guinier 1994; Singh 1998) or become so enmeshed with the party (Tate 2014) that they would have little power to effectively represent the interests of minorities. My research finds that minority legislators devote considerable effort, instead, to representing the full scope of civil rights organizations' policy priorities—while the organizations themselves have to limit their efforts primarily to the civil rights arena.

Civil Rights Organizations' Representation of Latino Interests

As discussed in chapter 3, Latino civil rights organizations are effective in representing Latino interests. Latinos list the economy, health care, and immigration as top policy concerns. The importance of immigration, particularly, has grown among Latinos in recent years. The lobbying data show that groups such as UnidosUS and MALDEF have been responsive to the desire of Latinos to push the federal government to enact comprehensive immigration reform. In the 110th and 111th Congresses, the groups spent significant resources lobbying on immigration bills. They supported the DREAM Act and other legislation that would create a robust pathway to citizenship for undocumented immigrants. Despite the criticism of grassroots immigration groups that the major Latino organizations should do more to get the federal government to act on this issue, there is little doubt that UnidosUS and MALDEF both have been at the forefront of these debates.

Even though immigration has dominated much of the Latino agenda from 2006 to 2019, it is just one issue among many for which Latino civil rights groups have provided representation to the Latino community. Some Latino politics scholars have expressed concern that the focus on immigration could diminish attention to other issues important to Latinos, such as civil rights, health care, and education. Angelo Falcón, president of the National Institute for Latino Policy, put it this way:

> In less than a decade, the Latino civil rights agenda became transformed in fundamental ways. The focus became the 8 million or so Latinos who were undocumented, while the issues facing the other more than 50 million who are U.S. citizens faded into the background in the public discourse. Traditional civil rights issues like affirmative action, employment and housing discrimination, bilingual education, voting rights, poverty, etc. were still being pursued, but they now seemed a bit dated and not as urgent as they once were. In opinion polls, "immigration" replaced "race" and "discrimination" as subjects. Racial issues receded back to the Black and White binary as "immigration" now stood as the surrogate of "Latino" and "Hispanic." (Falcón 2014, 1–2)

There is some evidence to support Falcón's argument. In the 111th Congress, of the eighty-five bills lobbied on by UnidosUS, only one was in the

area of traditional civil rights, representing 1.1 percent of the group's legislative agenda. Conversely, UnidosUS lobbied on five bills in the immigration policy area, representing 5.8 percent of its lobbying agenda.

Although Congress devoted a significant proportion of its agenda to
health care in the 110th and 111th Congresses, lobbying on health care was
not a significant part of the legislative agenda of Latino civil rights organizations. In the 111th Congress, of the eighty-five bills lobbied by UnidosUS,
only three were in the health-care-policy area, or 3.5 percent of its agenda.

It is important to remember that Latino civil rights groups spend a great
deal of their time working on appropriations and testifying at hearings
about funding for Hispanic-serving institutions and job training programs.
UnidosUS advocates for funding for many of its affiliates that provide social services to Latino constituents, including health-care services and educational training. UnidosUS also advocates for funding to support these
critical social and health services, even as it does not devote the same level
of attention to advocating for health care as it does to immigration. Immigration similarly is the major focus of MALDEF's legislative agenda. The
group spends some time on health care and jobs, but its primary focus is
squarely on immigration. Perhaps this is to be expected, because immigration is treated as civil rights issue, and health care is not the major focus of
the organization. Given that health care is a top priority of Latinos, however, perhaps it should receive the same level of attention from Latino civil
rights organizations.

LULAC's advocacy efforts for Latinos at the federal level are difficult to
quantify. The group, which once opposed establishing rights for undocumented residents, has shifted its position to become a strong proponent of
immigration reform. Lobbying disclosure reports do not indicate LULAC's
advocacy efforts in immigration debates, however; the group has not filed
lobbying advocacy reports indicating that it lobbies on the issue, and its
representatives are rarely called to testify. A LULAC rep whom I interviewed
stated that executive director Brent Wilkes met frequently with Obama administration officials to solve the crisis of children from Central America
being detained at the border. Although the group supports immigration
rights, it came under heavy fire when its president indicated that LULAC
would support the border enforcement plan proposed by President Donald Trump. Trump's plan included building a wall between Mexico and
the United States along the border. LULAC members were angered, including Wilkes himself. The LULAC president later retracted his statement and
resigned. The organization does not advocate actively advocate in other
policy areas, such as health care and education.

It would be difficult for any one group to represent all the various interests of Latinos. Although the largest existing Latino civil rights organizations claim to represent the broad interests of Latinos, they are still primarily civil rights organizations, and civil rights issues dominate the focus of their efforts. Health care and education are important to Latinos, but the major Latino civil rights organizations do not seem to have the capacity to represent Latinos in these areas beyond the support they offer for appropriations to their affiliates. The strategy of infusing Congress with more black and Latino legislators might be understood, in this context, as a way for these groups to boost their own advocacy efforts beyond civil rights and ensure the representation of the broad policy interests of black and Latino communities.

Legislative Allies as Advocates for Black and Latino Interests

The party system offers some significant advantages to blacks and Latinos, especially when they are in the majority party. The majority party can set the legislative agenda and affect the likelihood of a bill's passage through the chamber. Party leadership can control the agenda by appointing loyal partisans to full committee and subcommittee chairs. The Democratic Party is no longer overwhelmingly white, and it no longer includes among its members conservative Southern Democrats unwilling to address racial issues. Indeed, black and Latino legislators hold key positions in Democratic Party agenda setting and leadership. Black and Latino legislators are overwhelmingly in the Democratic Party, so when Democrats hold the House majority, civil rights groups benefit the most. In the 94th Congress (1975–1976), blacks and Latinos represented only 7.5 percent (22 of 291) of the Democratic delegation; in the 116th Congress (2019–2020) they represented 37.8 percent (89 of 235) of the delegation and 60 percent of Democratic Party leadership.[1] Black and Latino legislators serve as leaders of important committees that affect black and Latino interests. To get important legislation passed, Democrats must take into the account the preferences of CBC and CHC members. These groups have also formed coalitions with Asian Americans and white progressives. Thus, the political context has changed dramatically since Lani Guinier argued in 1994 that black legislators would have difficulty forming coalitions and would be pushed to the margins.

Examining how much resources groups spend on lobbying is an important measure of advocacy, but it provides an incomplete picture. Once elected, minority advocates can decrease the amount of resources necessary to receive effective representation of civil rights groups' policy interests in Congress. CBC members are forceful advocates for minority interests. Members of the CBC testified at hearings more frequently than did representatives of the top three civil rights organizations combined. The rise of the CBC coincides with the decline of testimony, or a flat rate of testimony, by civil rights groups. The normative implication is that blacks are getting more coverage. Still, more coverage is not necessarily equivalent to effective representation—especially if the CBC is restrained by party interests and its members are not as radical as they should be.

Disadvantages of Relying on Legislative Allies as Advocates

Although relying on legislative allies such as black and Latino legislators to push civil rights group interests in Congress has advantages, there are limitations for black and Latino advocacy. Some concerns of minority advocacy groups is that minority legislators have become too invested in being "team players" in the Democratic Party and that this association mitigates their ability to bring about the progressive policy change sought by civil rights groups. Even though black and Latino legislators rate highly on the NAACP, LCCR, and NHLA voting score reports, black and Latino politicians are not in lockstep with political advocacy groups. Although both groups claim to represent the interests of all blacks and Latinos, minority members of Congress are politicians, not civil rights activists.

Even the strategy used to increase the number of black and Latino legislators in Congress demonstrated the divisions between legislators and civil rights activists. In the 1990s redistricting process in North Carolina and Georgia, for example, the NAACP and ACLU wanted to maximize the number of black-majority seats drawn, but black Democratic legislators did not want to do so if it meant hurting the Democratic Party's chances of maintaining its majority in the Congress or in state legislatures (Davidson and Grofman 1994). Black and Latino legislators' need to balance the needs of the party against the demands of activists might limit how much they can fight for radical changes in the legislative process.

The CBC and CHC are also constrained by the policy objectives of the Democratic Party and party competition for control of Congress. The desire of Democrats to main majority status may moderate the policies pursued by black and Latino legislators. Although the Democratic Party is more attuned to minority interests than it once was, the party's necessary focus on reelection means that it is most attracted to issues supported by moderate to conservative voters, who are less likely to favor minority policy interests.

In an effort to get the Affordable Care Act passed, for example, Democrats did not include provisions favored by progressives, such as using a single-payer system and expanding Medicare and Medicaid programs. Similarly, Democratic presidential nominee Hilary Clinton was warned by some campaign officials to stay away from supporting Black Lives Matter for fear of alienating white voters.

Katherine Tate (2014) has argued the CBC has become less radical in promoting blacks' rights as it has become an important part of the Democratic Party. Tate's theory of concordance argues that as CBC members have gained more power through party leadership positions, their views have become more moderate. According to Tate, black lawmakers vote more frequently with the Democratic Party than they did in the past, and this generates symbolic and material benefits to blacks without addressing systemic and institutional effects of racial inequality. The party unity scores for black Democrats were 81 in 1977 compared to 97 in 2010. Thus, she argues, black legislators are more concerned about party interests than about addressing progressive policies that benefit blacks. At the same time, Tate finds that the Democratic Party itself became more liberal on racial issues and other issues supported by blacks. Tate argues that the trade-off is that the radical critique of social policies is left to social movements and interest groups. Black legislators used to factor into this critique, but they no longer do. The problem for interest groups is that they rely increasing on minority legislators as advocates for black interests—a strategy that her data suggests is increasingly wrongheaded.

The main limitation to Tate's critique for the purposes of this study lies in how she defines "radical policies," which she equates to policies that fall outside of the liberal-conservative continuum. She labels as radical such bills as the full employment legislation supported by Rep. Augustus Hawkins (D-CA) and Sen. Hubert Humphrey (D-MN), as well as the legislation against apartheid in Rhodesia and South Africa. According to Tate's own definition, black legislators have continued to support radical policies. They also have supported policies to eliminate the sentencing disparities between crack and powder cocaine—an issue that is considered of the far left but not necessarily outside the left-right spectrum. The CBC continues to support an alternative budget that does not differ too much from those of the 1970s. It is difficult using roll-call voting scores to tell in the absolute sense whether blacks have become more moderate or whether that apparent moderation is in fact an effect of the Democratic Party's having become more liberal. My findings show evidence of concordance, but the CBC remains a distinctive voice for black advocacy groups. These organizations' issues are no longer on the margins of the Democratic Party, because blacks constitute a powerful and cohesive voting bloc in the party. The CBC testified and lobbied on the legislative priorities of civil rights groups alongside the NAACP and the LCCR. The presence of more black and Latino legislators on committees, especially the House Judiciary Committee, led to more opportunities for these groups to participate.

Racial profiling and police brutality are concerns that still do not rise to the level of issues for the mainstream, although they have a place in the left-right continuum. Civil rights groups, along with black legislators, nonetheless push Congress to take steps to address these issues. Civil rights organizations protested to gain inclusion in the system, but that does not mean they have stopped advocating for non-mainstream policy like the payment of reparations to the descendants of slaves, a policy supported by leftists that Rep. John Conyers introduced to Congress for many consecutive years. Perhaps concordance has occurred, then, but that does not mean black legislators are providing less effective representation to their constituents or that they are failing to solve problems that affect the black community. Indeed, Tate acknowledges this point, but her book nonetheless assumes that less radical policies lead to less effective representation.

Regardless of which political party controls the federal government, civil rights organizations have been frustrated in their efforts to get Congress to pass comprehensive immigration reform and address racial profiling. The election of Republican Donald Trump to the U.S. presidency brings a new challenge to advocacy organizations seeking to advance the interests of black and Latino Americans. Unlike most contemporary U.S. presidents, Trump is openly hostile to Latino and black interests. For instance, in 2019, Trump claimed that he would deport more than one million undocumented immigrants. This followed his pledge to erect a border wall between the United States and Mexico. Trump and the GOP shut down the government for thirty-four days over their demand that Congress provide funding for the border wall.[2] Minority civil rights organizations do not expect the Trump administration or the GOP to support immigration reform, considering that Latinos vote overwhelmingly for the Democratic Party, but Democrats had an excellent opportunity to address immigration reform during the 111th Congress (2009–2010), when they had control of the House, Senate, and presidency, and they failed to do so. Obama, along with House Speaker Pelosi and Senate Majority Leader Reid, stated that Congress would not address immigration during the session. This was disappointing to many civil rights leaders, particularly leaders at UnidosUS, LULAC, and MALDEF, because black and Latino legislators held key positions in party leadership and on committees to influence the legislative agenda.

What was even more disturbing to these groups was the Obama administration's increased enforcement action at Immigration Customs and Enforcement (ICE) to deport undocumented immigrants. According to many reports, the Obama administration deported more immigrants than any other presidential administration had to date.[3] This led UnidosUS's president Janet Murguia to refer to Obama as the "deporter-in-chief": "For the president, I think his legacy is at stake here. We consider him the deportation president, or the deporter-in-chief."[4] This established a frosty relationship between the Obama administration and UnidosUS. Congressional Democrats, including the CHC, did not conduct hearings to question the president about ICE's increased enforcement efforts. Despite the overwhelming support Latinos provided to Democrats in the presidential and congressional elections in 2008 and 2010, their concerns regarding immigration went unaddressed. Legislative allies such as the CHC and the Congressional Tri-Caucus stood helpless as the issue languished in Congress. Immigration did not receive the attention that Latino civil rights groups thought it deserved, and it seems unlikely under the current administration that the issue will be addressed in a way that favors the priorities of Latino civil rights organizations.

Democrats did address health-care reform. In survey polls, Latinos have consistently identified access to health care as a top priority, in many cases ranking it a higher priority than immigration reform. Health care is listed consistently as an issue important to Latinos, but it was not the top priority of Latino civil rights advocacy groups. House Democrats introduced the minority health bill, which received a markup but did not become law. None of the provisions of the bill was incorporated into the Affordable Care Act (ACA). Other provisions related to minority health were incorporated into the ACA, however, as a result of advocacy by mainstream groups and minority legislators. The ACA created offices of minority health in many federal agencies, such as U.S. Department of Health and Human Services, the Food and Drug Administration, the Centers for Disease Control and Prevention, and the Substance Abuse and Mental Health Services Administration.

Black civil rights organizations wanted Congress under President Obama to pass a bill that would address black unemployment, which was a more significant problem than white unemployment. Congress passed a stimulus package that addressed some of the issues supported by the NAACP and NUL, but in a general sense, not much happened in Washington. The election of President Obama and the Democratic victory in

Congress brought much hope to civil rights organizations, but ultimately Democratic control of both Congress and the presidency provided only muted opportunities for advocacy to civil rights organizations—in part because congressional Democrats and the Obama administration feared that strong support for the policy preferences of civil rights groups would hurt their chances of reelection. Instead, they pursued policies that fit the median preferences of constituents.

The Polarization Problem

Party politics might be a means to achieving political success for civil rights groups, but the rise of party polarization limits expectations of how much progressive change of the type civil rights organizations favor the Congress is actually capable of enacting. As the Democratic Party has responded to the diversity of members in the party by devoting more attention to minority-interest issues, the GOP has become more conservative and less responsive to minority interests. The ability to forge bipartisan coalitions to pass progressive legislation like the Civil Rights Act of 1964 and the Voting Rights Act of 1965 has become increasingly impaired. In the 110th Congress (2007–2008), the rise of the Tea Party and, correspondingly, the Freedom Caucus in Congress pushed even moderate Republicans to the right, and party leaders were unwilling to compromise on bipartisan legislation. Indeed, attempts to compromise even affected the reelection chances of some legislators. In the Senate, for example, the "Gang of Eight" formed to craft a bipartisan immigration reform bill, and former U.S. House Majority Leader Eric Cantor (R-VA) supported immigration reform in the House. Cantor lost his seat in a primary to a conservative Republican who ran against immigration reform. Correspondingly, the rise of the liberal wing of the Democratic Party has pushed Democrats away from accepting compromise on bills once considered opportunities for bipartisan compromise, such as budget bills.

Although political parties have been reluctant to cede ground on policy for fear of losing important base voters, there remains some hope of bipartisan progress even in the context of either fierce competition to win the House or Senate majority or intense fear of losing it (Lee 2009, 2016). In the 115th Congress (2017–2018), Sen. Tim Scott (R-SC) worked with congressional Democrats to pass the Sickle-Cell Surveillance and Treatment Act in a Republican-controlled Congress. Democrats also worked closely with Sen. Orrin Hatch (R-UT) in the 111th Congress (2009–2010) to reduce sentencing disparities. There continues to be hope that Democrats and

Republicans can work together on major legislation, including legislation important to minority civil rights organizations and minority interests.

Hashtag Movements and the Future of Civil Rights Advocacy

Social movements and social movement organizations have played an important role in securing civil and political rights for women and minorities. The rise of so-called hashtag movements like Black Lives Matter and #MeToo seems to introduce a new trend toward movements without corresponding organizations. Social media giants such as Twitter and Facebook have been used by organizers of and participants in these movements to bring greater attention to issues like police brutality and sexual violence against women. It is unclear whether such social media campaigns have the ability to bring about substantive policy change in Congress, however. As discussed in chapter 3, Black Lives Matter is not a formal political organization and does not have much in the way of organizational strength. The group does not have an active membership, does not report formally lobbying members of Congress, and does not send representatives to testify at congressional hearings. When Rep. John Conyers (D-MI) introduced bills before Congress to address racial profiling, no one from Black Lives Matter testified at the hearing on the bill or submitted a letter to the hearing record. Several members of the CBC mentioned the movement as a reason for drawing attention to the issue, however.

What remains unclear is how traditional civil rights organizations and political parties can use the awareness raised by these hashtag movements to advance their policy goals on behalf of underrepresented groups. Do hashtag movements push traditional groups to move certain issues higher on their legislative agenda? Similarly, the NAACP lobbied on fair pay for women but not on issues that pertain more directly to minority women, such as violence against women. These traditional groups continue to take a single-axis approach, with racial issues still dominating their advocacy agenda (Brown 2014; Hancock 2004).

Threats to the VRA

The U.S. House of Representatives is one of the most racially and ethnically diverse elite institutions in the United States. The House is more diverse than the U.S. Senate, most major private corporations, and predominantly white universities and colleges. Long-term political pressure from racial and ethnic minorities alongside white liberals has made it this way. The

VRA brought about significant demographic changes in the House. In 2010, the percentage of blacks in the U.S. population stood at 12.6 percent, or 38.9 million—roughly the same as it was in 1970, when it was 11.1 percent, or 22.5 million—but in 1970, only 2 percent of House representatives, or ten members, were black, whereas by 2010 the proportion of black representatives in the House had increased to 9.2 percent, or forty-one members, due in part to redistricting (Gibson and Jung 2002). For Latinos, in contrast, the population shift has been significant. In 1970, Latinos represented only 4.7 percent of the U.S. population, or 9.5 million people. By 2010, they accounted for 16.3 percent of the population, or 50.4 million people (Humes, Jones, and Ramirez 2011). Only five Latinos served in the House in 1970, making up 1 percent of representatives, but by 2010, twenty-nine Latino members served in the House, 6.5 percent of the total House membership. Although some blacks and Latinos have been successfully elected in majority-white districts, the vast majority of black and Latino legislators come from majority-minority districts. In 2011, 75 percent of black legislators and 63 percent of Latino legislators in the House were elected from majority-minority districts. This shift resulted from a long-running strategy by civil rights organizations to use diversity to bring about legislative change and to protect the legislative gains of the 1960s. The preponderance of the evidence shows that demographic changes alone would not have led to this level of diversity in Congress (Davidson and Grofman 1994).

Yet recent challenges to the VRA have made it increasingly difficult to create majority-minority districts. In *Shelby County v. Holder* (2013), the U.S. Supreme Court changed the coverage formula and significantly weakened Section 5, the preclearance provision of the VRA. Under the preclearance provision, the Department of Justice (DOJ) is charged with reviewing any changes to the voting plans of covered jurisdictions, which are mainly southern states that have a demonstrated history of hindering and diluting the voting strength of racial and ethnic minorities. The DOJ review process includes examining states' redistricting plans to ensure that state government entities do not engage in crafting districts that dilute minority strength and hinder the ability of racial and ethnic minorities to elect a candidate of their choice. Chief Justice Roberts, writing for the court majority, stated that the preclearance provision was no longer necessary because the discriminatory conditions in the South that had prevented minorities from voting no longer existed.

The Supreme Court's willingness to weaken the VRA diminishes opportunities for blacks and Latinos to gain additional representation in Congress, especially in fast-growing regions like the South and Southwest.

According to data gathered by the Texas Demographic Center, from 2000 to 2010, the population of Texas increased from 20.8 million to 25.1 million people.[5] Blacks and Latinos were the main drivers of this population growth. Together, blacks and Latinos represented 77 percent of the state's population gain, or 3.1 million people. As a result of its population growth, Texas gained four additional seats in the U.S. House. Yet only one of the new seats drawn by Texas's Republican-controlled legislature consisted of a majority-black or majority-Latino district. Because the Texas redistricting occurred before *Shelby v. Holder*, Texas had to get its maps precleared by the DOJ or district court. And because Democrats controlled the Department of Justice and likely would have ordered Texas to redraw districts in a way that would be more favorable to black and Latino voters, the state bypassed the DOJ and went to the district court. In 2011, black and Latino civil rights organizations filed suit in federal district court, arguing the Texas state legislature drew legislative districts that violated the VRA by failing to create majority-black and majority-Latino districts. The district court ruled in favor of the civil rights groups and ordered the state of Texas to redraw its maps. The state then appealed the lower court's decision to the Supreme Court. In *Abbott v. Perez* (2018), the court reversed the lower court's decision and ruled that the state legislature's congressional redistricting map did not violate the rights of black and Latino voters. This represented another setback to black and Latino civil rights groups seeking to increase their numbers and legislative allies in the House.

Subsequent to these rulings, civil rights groups have directed their focus to striking down partisan gerrymandered districts, especially in states where GOP-dominated state legislatures have constructed districts to disadvantage the election of Democratic candidates. Although the U.S. Supreme Court has thus far maintained the constitutionality of partisan gerrymandering, civil rights organizations have argued that gerrymandered districts limit the ability of racial and ethnic minorities to receive representation, thus violating the equal protection clause of the Fourteenth Amendment. The Republican Party has significant partisan majorities in state legislatures and has used this power to draw lines favorable to the election of GOP candidates in state and federal legislative elections. As many political representation studies demonstrate, GOP majorities do not advance the substantive representation of minority civil rights organizations or the people they represent (Minta and Sinclair-Chapman 2013). Although the effort to end partisan redistricting might benefit minority civil rights groups in the short term, it is not clear if it would do much to increase the number of blacks and Latinos in Congress. Black and Latino legislators are primarily Democrats, and they have increased their influence in the party and in state legislatures. Efforts to diminish the power of state legislatures to draw districts might result in diminished power for these groups. Thus, plans to shift this power from legislatures to independent redistricting commissions should examine the impact that doing so would have on the ability of states to create majority-minority districts. Finally, policy makers and legislators should work toward restoring the power of the preclearance provision of the VRA to allow the U.S. Department of Justice to review plans by jurisdictions that may have an impact on the ability of minority citizens to elect the candidates of their choice.

Reliance on Corporate Donors

Civil rights organizations rely primarily on contributions from affluent individuals, corporations, and foundations to fund their advocacy activities. These corporate and foundation contributions have increased the organizational capacity of civil rights groups, allowing them to remain an active force in the advocacy community on behalf of minorities. In fact, civil rights groups rely more than ever before on outside funding. In 2015, for instance, the NAACP's revenue of $27.4 million was more than three times its 1964 revenue of $8.7 million (in 2015 dollars), but 59 percent of the 2015 revenue came from corporate and foundation donors, compared to only 6 percent in 1964.[6] As discussed in chapter 3, it is possible that heavy reliance on corporate and foundation funding may moderate the activism of civil rights organizations to meet the policy objectives of funding organizations (Haines 1984; Marquez 2003). Outside funding may also influence a shift in the role of civil rights organizations from political advocates to social service providers (Minkoff 1999). Large corporations such as AT&T, Wells Fargo, and Walmart, all of which have provided funding to civil rights organizations, nonetheless spend most of their political dollars supporting Republican candidates and policies that are not aligned with the interests of black and Latino Americans. Thus, many scholars are skeptical that civil rights groups that receive corporate money can sufficiently represent minority interests.

In chapter 3, I found that the receipt of large contributions by AT&T, UPS, and Wells Fargo have not thus far diminished the scope of civil rights organizations' advocacy for minority interests. Civil rights organizations focus their efforts on advocating for civil rights, social welfare, and immigration—all issues that are important to blacks and Latinos. This result is understandable when we consider that corporations and foundations claim to give money to civil rights organizations because they support some aspect of their charitable work, not necessarily because they back the groups' legislative agendas. Civil rights leaders are offended, moreover, at the suggestion that funding from outside groups could affect their policy positions or legislative agendas. Supporters of net neutrality, for example, have argued that LULAC and the NAACP's opposition to net neutrality was a position largely driven by donations these groups received from large telecommunications companies, but the leaders of LULAC and the NAACP have denied this accusation. Brent Wilkes, executive director of LULAC, explained, "We take our stance based on what we believe are the best interests of the Latino community, and we have not been pressured by these companies."[7]

Again, the evidence does not show that LULAC or the NAACP are devoting much time to advocating in the telecommunications policy area. However, there is a need for future research to examine the policy battles that civil rights groups may not enter from fear of upsetting corporate contributors. Researchers should also look at the intensity of their advocacy efforts. Although civil rights groups appear to devote significant effort to issues considered important to minorities, the issues that receive the most funding from outside sources may get the most attention, while other issues may not receive the same level of attention from organization leaders.

Final Considerations

Advocacy on the Hill is a process shrouded in secrecy and surrounded by public pronouncements in the media and from the general citizenry of corruption and undue influence. Lobbying is considered a province reserved for special and narrow interests. In 2008, U.S. presidential candidate Barack Obama pledged not to accept campaign donations from lobbyists. Obama also said he would support legislation that banned government officials from joining lobbying firms similar to the ones on K Street. Even though Congress has done much to make lobbying and advocacy on the Hill more transparent, the general public still knows very little and is suspicious about lobbying and its specific aims. Working in this environment, advocacy groups do not even consider much of what they do to be lobbying. It is difficult for interest group members to assess whether civil rights organizations are doing much to help them.

Despite all the negative connotations associated with lobbying, lobbying is the major way other than elections in which citizens, through organized groups, communicate their policy preferences to lawmakers. Lobbying is not just the province of large lobbying firms on K Street representing corporate interests; it also consists of in-house advocates in small nonprofit organizations that work on shoestring budgets. Even before the civil rights movement, black and Latino organizations engaged in this insider game waged mostly outside of the view of the general public. Most accounts of civil rights advocacy focus on the litigation efforts of civil rights groups in cases such as *Brown v. Board of Education*. Even greater attention was devoted to grassroots action led by SCLC president Martin Luther King Jr. to protest segregation in the South, or César Chávez spearheading protests for the rights of farmworkers. Yet such events are not the main type of work done by the advocacy community. In fact, most of the advocacy efforts of the NAACP throughout its 110-year-plus history have relied mainly on insider tactics.

In fact, the founding fathers in the *Federalist Papers* envisioned a pluralist system that is present today in American society. To protect against majority tyranny in government, groups form to represent the interests of all members of society. These organizations comprise diverse interests and cannot possibly form factions to take control of government and make policies adverse to a minority. Although pluralism is far from perfect, the interests of marginalized groups are represented by professional organizations that actively lobby on Capitol Hill. These groups have strong membership bases, such as those of the NAACP and LULAC, that help them determine the needs of blacks and Latinos. They also comprise service providers such as UnidosUS and NUL that are actively working in communities to address specific needs. These civil rights organizations have experienced and professional staff who have developed strong reputations with legislators on Capitol Hill. They are regularly called to testify at congressional hearings and do important work in the policy-making process. Civil rights groups played a significant role in increasing their influence in Congress by helping create a diverse House of Representatives through their efforts in redistricting. Not only does this diversity lead to more opportunities to testify, but legislation supported by civil rights organizations has a greater likelihood of receiving attention from congressional committees than it once did.

Black and Latino civil rights organizations continue to negotiate the delicate balance between the fierce advocacy for liberal policies demanded by their constituents and the necessity of working within a political system that protects the status quo through incremental change. They also work in a system that requires substantial resources to maintain an active and consistent lobbying presence on Capitol Hill. As a result, they are consistently open to criticism that they are not doing enough to represent minority interests or that their advocacy is compromised and not representative of the community. The expectation that civil rights groups are not effective because they have failed to push Congress to enact immigration reform or anti–racial profiling measures may not be an appropriate or fair way to assess advocacy success of civil rights organizations. Existing research shows that minority groups rarely win in the federal policy arena and that Congress responds primarily to the interests of the wealthy (Griffin and Newman 2008; Bartels 2008). Congress does not spend much time on civil rights or social welfare issues compared to other issue areas, even in the decades since minority representation at the federal level has improved. Most of what Congress does is fund government programs. Having civil rights organizations and black and Latino legislators at the table to fight for government funding might be a worthwhile even if these groups lose more often than they win.

Despite the fairness of the critiques of traditional civil rights organizations from activists in the Black Lives Matter and #MeToo social movements, these activists force traditional civil rights groups to actively engage different forms of communication to ensure they are reaching a younger generation. Combining traditional advocacy tools with new social media platforms may do more to draw attention and participation from different segments of the minority community into the agenda-setting process of minority civil rights groups. Some civil rights organizations have already started to address these issues, but more can be done to ensure that civil rights groups are responsive to needs of black and Latinos in the twenty-first century and beyond.

ACKNOWLEDGMENTS

Writing an academic book is no small task. Although I authored this book alone, many individuals provided vital support that enabled me to complete this project. I thank my wife, Janell, for accompanying me on this life journey. While helping with our kids and managing her career, she still had time and patience to provide the encouragement necessary to allow me to finish this book. Her presence makes my life richer and happier. My children, Kendall, Braden, Bryson, and Preston, remind me that there is much more to life than just work and career responsibilities. They are smart, beautiful, and funny. I love them so much, and they inspire me to be a better person and dad. My parents, Dorothy and David Johnson, continue to provide unconditional love and support for me and my family. They were the first to believe in me, even before I believed in myself. Thanks for always loving and being there for me. My sister, Tosha Nettles, and my brother, David Johnson III, have always been there for me. They provide love, support, and advice for me. I thank my in-laws, Esther and Spurgeon Lofton, Adrienne Lofton Kumekpor, and Meshelle Lofton, for the unwavering support and love they provide our family. I am truly blessed to have them in my life.

I want to thank my colleagues who have supported me and this project from the beginning. There are not enough words in this section to describe what Frank Baumgartner has meant to this project and to me. He asks the tough questions and pushes me to think deeper, and the result is a much better product—and I am a much better scholar. He believed in me when many others did not. I am happy to call him my colleague and friend. I also thank Jeffrey Berry, David Canon, Christian Grose, Kathryn Pearson, Valeria Sinclair-Chapman, Dara Strolovitch, and Sophia Wallace for reading and providing feedback on different iterations of this project.

They helped shape and guide this project. I would like to thank the participants in a Rice University workshop organized by Leslie Schwindt Bayer and Matthew Hayes for their helpful comments. Likewise, I want to thank the participants at the conference held by the Center for Effective Lawmaking organized by Craig Volden and Alan Wiseman for their comments. I appreciate the excellent editorial support provided by Ruth Homrighaus and Leanne Powner. Ruth assisted me with my first book many years ago, and I am so happy she came out of retirement in time to assist me again. She is truly amazing at what she does.

The data collection and expert analysis of my team of research assistants made it possible to complete a project of this magnitude. I thank the excellent graduate students who assisted me on this project, Avram Munoz and Hannah McVeigh. I thank the talented undergraduate students Yemaya Hanna, John Bradley, Eva Chen, Max Chu, Melissa Hill, Kyle Tepper, Giselle Webber, Taylor Bushelle, Christina Laridaen, Anna Baish, and Alicia Guler, who worked on this project through the University of Minnesota's Dean's First Year Research and Creative Scholars Program and the Department of Political Science's Distinguished Undergraduate Research Internship Program. Additionally, I thank Dana Angello and Myunghee Lee for their research assistance when I was at the University of Missouri. I also want to acknowledge the University of Minnesota's Talle Faculty Grant and the University of Missouri's Research Board for generously funding this project.

Finally, I would like to thank Charles Myers at the University of Chicago Press for guiding me through the editorial process. Chuck has believed in this project and has provided wonderful guidance throughout the process. Thanks for believing in this project and in me.

CHAPTER ONE

1. NAACP Papers, box X, Manuscripts Division, Library of Congress, Washington, DC.
2. Information for the USCC and major civil rights organizations such as the NAACP, LCCR, and UnidosUS was obtained from the Center for Responsive Politics, https://www.opensecrets.org/orgs/all-profiles (accessed June 16, 2020).
3. Again, information for the USCC and major civil rights organizations such as the NAACP, LCCR, and UnidosUS was obtained from the Center for Responsive Politics, https://www.opensecrets.org/orgs/all-profiles (accessed June 16, 2020).
4. This quote is Shelton's "favorite quote" at the oral history website The History-Makers. See "Hilary Shelton," HistoryMakers, https://www.thehistorymakers.org/biography/hilary-shelton-44.
5. I do not suggest that civil rights groups failed to achieve any success with less diversity in Congress. In fact, the narrative claiming that Congress did little to address minority civil rights ignores the long arc of advocacy by these groups.
6. House and Senate bills (HR and S, respectively) are used to calculate the total. Joint and concurrent resolutions are excluded from this total. Specifically, I calculated the hearings and markups held in the House by limiting my search to all hearings held on all House bills (HR) introduced during the 110th Congress. This can be done in the Congress.gov database by selecting the specific congressional period and selecting "House committee/subcommittee hearings and markups" under "Action and Status." The data come from the website Congress.gov, accessed August 14, 2019.
7. The availability of lobbying disclosure reports to examine limits how far I can analyze legislative success of civil rights groups. The Center for Responsive Politics' database on lobbying activity, which ranges from 1999 to 2018, or the 106th Congress to the 115th Congress), contains only two Congresses in which Democrats were in control of the House—the 110th and 111th Congresses. I attempted a similar analysis for legislative success for the congresses in the 1970s and 1980s. I collected lobbying disclosure reports for several groups at the National Archives and at university libraries. The main problem encountered with collecting information on early periods is that groups rarely submitted lobbying disclosure reports, and when they did, they did not always identify the specific bills on which they lobbied. For example, I did not find lobbying reports submitted by UnidosUS or LULAC during the 1970s

and 1980s. The NAACP's lobbying disclosure reports would not always list bills on which they lobbied. Although there is value in assessing minority legislators' efforts to keep legislation off the agenda that hurt minority interests, especially when Republicans control the House, I focus mainly on positive agenda activity.

CHAPTER TWO

1. In addition to the NAACP and NUL, a number of other civil rights groups advocate for the rights of black Americans, including the LCCR and the Lawyers' Committee for Civil Rights under Law. The LCCR was established in 1950, and it initially spent considerable effort lobbying for civil rights for black Americans. Since 1970, however, the LCCR has become firmly established as an umbrella group that addresses a wide variety of interests.

2. Weiss (1974) notes that it is difficult to tell how much advocacy the NUL did before the 1940s because of many of the NUL records were either lost or destroyed when the organization changed headquarters.

3. Calculated by the author using data from www.congress.gov, accessed August 14, 2019.

4. Calculated by the author using data from www.congress.gov, accessed August 14, 2019.

5. Calculated by the author using DW-NOMINATE scores that measure legislators' ideological positions.

6. In a study by the Social Security Administration, DeWitt (2010) refutes this argument.

7. In 2017, the NCLR changed its name again to UnidosUS. The UnidosUS president Janet Murguia stated that the name better represented the changing demographics of the Latino community. "We are UnidosUS," UnidosUS, news release, July 10, 2017, https://www.unidosus.org/about-us/media/press/releases/071117-Rebranding -Release.

8. Missing in her account is the role of the Congressional Hispanic Caucus in working with Latino groups to push immigration-specific legislation.

9. Calculated by the author using information from Jason Windett and Mary Layton Atkinson, 2018, "Cong88-110_Amended.dta," replication data on congressional bills for Gender Stereotypes and the Policy Priorities of Women in Congress, 2018, https://doi.org/10.7910/DVN/IJEWYV/K2JUUJ, Harvard Dataverse, V.2.

10. Lani Guinier (1994, 41) called this the "theory of black electoral success," and she had little hope that it would change the fortunes of blacks. It was not just blacks who wanted more minority legislators, however; many Latino groups also wanted more Latino legislators in Congress.

11. Calculated by the author using data from Jeffrey B. Lewis, Keith Poole, Howard Rosenthal, Adam Boche, Aaron Rudkin, and Luke Sonnet, *Voteview: Congressional Roll-Call Votes Database*, 2020, https://voteview.com.

12. In-person interview with Luis Torres, LULAC, Director of Policy and Legislation, July 30, 2014.

13. Don Shannon, "Hispanic Caucus of 5 Opens Its Doors," *Los Angeles Times*, June 2, 1977 (ProQuest Historical Newspapers).

14. The Democrats controlled the House in following Congresses: 103rd (1993–1994), 110th (2007–2008), 111th (2009–2010), and 116th (2019–2020).

CHAPTER THREE

1. Melissa Harris-Perry, "How to Save the N.A.A.C.P. from Irrelevance," *New York Times*, May 30, 2017, https://www.nytimes.com/2017/05/30/opinion/melissa-harris-perry-naacp.html.

2. "Opinion: Latinos Need a Voice. Where Is It?" NBC News, June 19, 2017, https://www.nbcnews.com/think/news/opinion-latinos-need-voice-where-it-ncna771701.

3. "Nation's Premier Civil Rights Organization," NAACP, https://www.naacp.org/nations-premier-civil-rights-organization/; "About Us," LULAC, https://www.lulac.org/about/.

4. Phone interview with Carol Kaplan, congressional analyst, NAACP, July 9, 2014.

5. In-person interview with Hilary Shelton, director of the NAACP's Washington Bureau and senior vice president for advocacy and policy, NAACP, July 31, 2013.

6. "Local Affiliates," National Urban League, https://nul.org/local-affiliates.

7. "Key Issues, Washington Bureau," National Urban League, https://nul.org/washington-bureau.

8. In-person interviews with Charles Kamasaki, senior vice president of policy and advocacy, and Lisa Navarette, special adviser to the president, UnidosUS, August 1, 2013.

9. "Unidos US Affiliate Network," UnidosUS, February 12, 2020, https://www.unidosus.org/affiliates.

10. In-person interviews with Kamasaki and with Navarette, August 1, 2013.

11. The IRS and the National Center for Charitable Statistics use the National Taxonomy of Exempt Entities (NTEE) to classify nonprofit organizations into major categories that relate to the function and goals of the organizations. These categories focus on issue areas, such as health, education, and human services.

12. LULAC is a 501(c)(4) organization, but it also has a 501(c)(3) entity, LULAC National Educational Service Centers, which in 2015 had $5.6 million in gross receipts.

13. National Association for the Advancement of Colored People, and Historical Society of Pennsylvania, *NAACP 1964 Annual Report*. The revenue was $1.1 million in 1964 dollars.

14. In 1968, UnidosUS was founded by a grant from the Ford Foundation. Unlike the NAACP, the organization has always had the 501(c)(3) designation. Revenue data for 1969 found in an April 23, 1982, memo to Technical Assistance and Constituency Support Committee Members, National Council of La Raza (UnidosUS), by Arnoldo Resendez, acting vice president of the Technical Assistance and Constituency Support Committee included in the board minutes, October 6–9, 1983. Call Number M744, box 6, folder 5, National Council of La Raza, 1969, National Council of La Raza records, Stanford University, Stanford, CA.

15. Schlozman, Verba, and Brady (2012) employed a more refined classification system in their database than the broad categories established by NTEE. They identified specific groups that advocate for African Americans, Latinos, and other racial or ethnic groups.

16. Calculated by the author using lobbying expenditure data from the Center for Responsive Politics.

17. The ACLU frequently lobbies for minority interest issues, but the group is not devoted solely to the advancement of the interests of racial or ethnic minorities.

18. The Lobbying Disclosure Act (1995) provides a narrow definition of lobbying activity. Lobbying is defined as activities designed to influence federal governmental officials; these activities can include meeting with legislators or writing letters to

get these legislators to support legislation favored by the advocacy organization. Civil rights groups regularly testify at public hearings, but this activity is not considered lobbying by the federal government, and groups do not have to report it on lobbying disclosure forms. The ability of groups to devote resources to lobbying gives them the best opportunity to be responsive to African American and Latino interests.

19. I converted the Center for Responsive Politics lobbying expenditures data for civil rights groups into 2016 dollars using the Consumer Price Index Inflation Calculator found at the website of the U.S. Bureau of Labor Statistics, https://data.bls.gov/cgi -bin/cpicalc.pl.

20. Groups might appear to be more active in the 2000s than in the 1970s because organizations have not been consistent in reporting their lobbying efforts. One of the top lobbyists for UnidosUS, Charles Kamasaki, said that the amount of activity reported in the LDRs reflects the compliance stage. According to Kamasaki, most groups, including UnidosUS, report more bills on the LDR than they did in the past because they do not want to run afoul of the LDA and get in trouble with the IRS. So groups might have been just as active in past years on issues but reported less lobbying because the LDA was not as stringent in terms of reporting requirements (interview with Kamasaki).

21. NAACP Lobby Disclosure Reports, 1969-1979, National Association for the Advancement of Colored People. *National Association for the Advancement of Colored People Records.* box IX:292, folders 1 and 2, NAACP, Baltimore. Bills introduced in the Congress obtained from the *Congressional Record–Daily Digest, Resume of Congressional Activity*, 1978 and 1979, http://library.clerk.house.gov/resume.aspx.

22. Time Series Cumulative Data File (1948–2016), American National Election Studies, https://electionstudies.org/data-center/anes-time-series-cumulative-data-file/.

23. Alyssa Brown, "Views of Race Relations as Top Problem Still Differ by Race," Gallup, June 11, 2015, https://news.gallup.com/poll/183572/race-divides-views-race -relations-top-problem.aspx.

24. "On Views of Race and Inequality, Blacks and Whites Are Worlds Apart," Social and Demographic Trends, Pew Research Center, June 27, 2016, https://www .pewsocialtrends.org/2016/06/27/on-views-of-race-and-inequality-blacks-and -whites-are-worlds-apart/.

25. See Luis R. Fraga, John A. Garcia, Rodney Hero, Michael Jones-Correa, Valerie Martinez-Ebers, and Gary M. Segura, *Latino National Survey (LNS), 2006* (ICPSR20862-v6), Inter-University Consortium for Political and Social Research [distributor], University of Michigan, June 5, 2013, http://doi.org/10.3886/ ICPSR20862.v6. Question wording matters in terms of the responses that Latinos give interviewers. When respondents were asked to state the most important problem facing the country, as opposed to the Latino community, the U.S. War in Iraq was respondents' top choice, followed by the economy and illegal immigration. The Iraq War, which overwhelmingly was mentioned as the most important problem facing the country, barely registered as a problem facing the community.

26. Jens Manuel Krogstad, "Top Issue for Hispanics? Hint: It's Not Immigration," *Fact Tank, News in the Numbers*, Pew Research Center, June 2, 2014, https://www .pewresearch.org/fact-tank/2014/06/02/top-issue-for-hispanics-hint-its-not -immigration/.

27. In-person interview with Lisa Navarette, Special Advisor to the President, UnidosUS, August 1, 2013.

28. "Justice Department Reaches Settlement with Wells Fargo Resulting in More Than $175 Million in Relief for Homeowners to Resolve Fair Lending Claims," US Department of Justice, July 12, 2012, https://www.justice.gov/opa/pr/justice-department -reaches-settlement-wells-fargo-resulting-more-175-million-relief.

CHAPTER FOUR

1. From 2001 to 2002, Republicans lost control of the Senate because Jim Jeffords (R-VT) switched from the GOP to Independent status, thus giving Democrats majority control of the Senate.

2. "Fair Housing, Spotlight: Predatory Lending," Avoice, African American Voices in Congress, http://www.avoiceonline.org/fair-housing/lending.html.

3. Civil rights organizations were successful in obtaining the passage of major civil rights legislation during the 1960s; however, much of this legislation came as a result of pressure applied to the federal government by civil rights protests. The aim of this study is to examine the degree of success of these organizations beyond the protest movements.

4. The National Hispanic Leadership Agenda's voting scorecard was not published for the 110th Congress. The NHLA keeps score only periodically on members' voting records.

5. I focus on black and Latino civil rights advocacy because these groups engaged in litigation to create majority-minority districts.

6. Because Democrats were in majority in the 95th and 111th Congresses, the party leadership positions included the Speaker of the House, Majority Leader, Majority Whip, and Democratic Caucus Chair.

7. House Foreign Affairs was the most diverse committee in the 110th Congress, which speaks to CBC and CHC interests on issues that relate to the Caribbean and Latin America. The CBC and CHC both have task forces that focus on the foreign affairs, where legislators serve concurrently on the task force and the House committee.

8. The 110th Congress and 111th Congress are analyzed to determine the legislative success of civil rights groups under divided and unified party control of government. Moreover, most civil rights groups' policy positions are aligned with those of the Democratic Party. Thus, if there is any success at all, it is likely to occur when Democrats have the ability to set the House agenda.

9. Legislative success is assessed by examining positive agenda-setting activity, or bills receiving a markup by a committee, under Democratic control of the House.

10. The NAACP lobbied on 108 distinct bills in 2007–2008, but some of the bills were referred to more than one committee. The bill committee match captures the multiple referrals of a single bill; thus, the bill committee match combination is 142 instead of 108. For example, sentencing disparity was referred to the House Judiciary and Education and Labor Committees. Although the same bill was referred to both committees, the bill was counted as two separate observations.

11. Specifically, I calculated the hearings held in the House by limiting my search to all hearings held on all House bills (HR) introduced during the 110th Congress. This can be done using the Congress.gov database by selecting the specific congressional period and under "Action and Status" selecting "House committee/subcommittee hearings."

12. Percentage calculated by author using data from the Library of Congress website Congress.gov.

13. In other models not reported here, I also controlled for racial and ethnic district

composition of committee members, and the results for diversity of the committee membership was still statistically significant.

14. The proportion of black legislators on the committee was not found to directly affect issues lobbied on by the NUL, but that result is most likely explained by the difficulty in estimating a small sample size of issues.

15. LULAC was not included in the multivariate committee analysis, primarily because it did not engage in significant lobbying on the federal level—that is, lobbying that could be captured through lobbying disclosure reports or an examination of witness testimony and statements at congressional hearings and markups.

16. I examine the bills that civil rights groups want to become law, not the bills and amendments these groups opposed. Efforts by organizations to keep bills and amendments harmful to the organizations' constituents off the congressional agenda are not included and do not bias the results. Getting positive action on legislation is much more difficult to accomplish than negative action. Thus, the model might understate the level of success of civil rights organizations in the legislative arena.

17. E. Scott Adler and John Wilkerson, Congressional Bills Project: 93rd to 114th Congresses, NSF grants 00880066 and 00880061, http://www.congressionalbills.org/download.html.

CHAPTER FIVE

1. U.S. Congress, House Committee on Ways and Means (1935).

2. Calculated by the author using witness testimony data from ProQuest Congressional. This is a searchable database that provides information on all individuals and groups that testify before Congress.

3. Calculated by the author using hearings data from ProQuest Congressional and Policy Agendas Project Data.

4. Calculated by the author using hearings data from ProQuest Congressional and Policy Agendas Project Data.

5. Calculated by the author using hearings data from ProQuest Congressional and Policy Agendas Project Data.

6. Table 5.1 shows civil rights, social welfare, and immigration ranking in the bottom five of the twenty-one policy areas receiving hearings in the House.

7. NAACP, *NAACP Policy Handbook: Resolutions Approved by the National Board of Directors, 1976–2006*, https://www.naacp.org/wp-content/uploads/2018/07/Policy _Handbook_5_9_07-1.pdf.

8. A Pew Research poll conducted from 2004 to 2012 of Latino registered voters. Jens Manuel Krogstad, "Top Issue for Hispanics? Hint: It's Not Immigration," *Fact Tank, News in the Numbers*, Pew Research Center, June 2, 2014, https://www.pewresearch .org/fact-tank/2014/06/02/top-issue-for-hispanics-hint-its-not-immigration/.

9. "New Issues Likely to Emerge under Democrats," NBC News, November 22, 2006, http://www.nbcnews.com/id/15855225/ns/us_news-life/t/new-issues-likely-emerge -under-democrats/.

10. Data calculated by the author using data from ProQuest Congressional.

11. The Policy Agendas Project separates immigration from civil right issues, while civil rights organizations consider immigration to be part of their civil rights agenda. Considering that immigration hearings frequently deal with such matters as pathways to citizenship for immigrants, at least some immigration advocacy should clearly be included in the civil rights category.

12. "Uninsured Rates for the Nonelderly by Race/Ethnicity, State Health Facts," KFF, 2010, https://www.kff.org/uninsured/state-indicator/rate-by-raceethnicity/?current Timeframe=0&sortModel=%7B%22colId%22:%22Location%22,%22sort%22: %22asc%22%7D.

CHAPTER SIX

1. Calculated by the author using information obtained for the U.S. House Clerk's website (www.clerk.house.gov), accessed October 25, 2019.

2. Mihir Zaveri, Guilbert Gates, and Karen Zraick, "The Government Shutdown Was the Longest Ever: Here's the History," *New York Times*, January 9, 2019 (updated January 25, 2019), https://www.nytimes.com/interactive/2019/01/09/us/politics/ longest-government-shutdown.html.

3. Reid J. Epstein, "NCLR Head: Obama 'Deporter-in-Chief,'" *Politico*, March 4, 2014, https://www.politico.com/story/2014/03/national-council-of-la-raza-janet-murguia -barack-obama-deporter-in-chief-immigration-104217.

4. Epstein.

5. "Texas Population Projections 2010 to 2050," Texas Demographic Center, https:// demographics.texas.gov/Resources/publications/2019/20190128_PopProjections Brief.pdf.

6. Percentage calculated by the author using information obtained from the NAACP's 1964 and 2015 annual reports, the latter of which is available at https://www.naacp .org/wp-content/uploads/2018/07/NAACP2015AnnualReport.pdf.

7. Gerry Smith, "Why Is The NAACP Siding with Verizon over Net Neutrality?" *Huffington Post*, July 31, 2014, https://www.huffpost.com/entry/net-neutrality-naacp -verizon_n_5630074.

REFERENCES

Alexander, Michelle. 2010. *The New Jim Crow: Mass Incarceration in the Age of Colorblindness*. New York: New Press.

Anderson, Carol. 2003. *Eyes off the Prize: The United Nations and the African American Struggle for Human Rights, 1944–1955*. New York: Cambridge University Press.

Austen-Smith, David, and John R. Wright. 1994. "Counteractive Lobbying." *American Journal of Political Science* 38: 25–44.

Barnett, Marguerite Ross. 1982. The Congressional Black Caucus: Illusions and Realities of Power. In *The New Black Politics*, edited by Michael B. Preston, Lenneal J. Henderson, and Paul L. Puryear. New York: Longman.

Barreto, Matt and Gary M. Segura. 2014. *Latino America: How America's Most Dynamic Population Is Poised to Transform the Politics of the Nation*. New York: Public Affairs Books.

Bartels, Larry M. 2008. *Unequal Democracy: The Political Economy of the New Gilded Age*. Princeton, NJ: Princeton University Press.

Bartley, Tim. 2007. "How Foundations Shape Social Movements: The Construction of an Organizational Field and the Rise of Forest Certification Review." *Social Problem* 54: 229–55.

Bateman, David A., Ira Katznelson, and John S. Lapinski. 2018. *Southern Nation: Congress and White Supremacy after Reconstruction*. Princeton, NJ: Princeton University Press.

Bauer, Raymond A., Ithiel de Sola Pool, and Lewis A. Dexter. 1963. *American Business and Public Policy: The Politics of Foreign Trade*. New York: Atherton Press.

Baumgartner, Frank R., Jeffrey M. Berry, Marie Hojnacki, David C. Kimball, and Beth L. Leech. 2009. *Lobbying and Policy Change: Who Wins, Who Loses, and Why*. Chicago: University of Chicago Press.

Baumgartner, Frank R., and Bryan D. Jones. 1993. *Agendas and Instability in American Politics*. Chicago: University of Chicago Press.

Baumgartner, Frank R., and Bryan D. Jones. 2002. "Positive and Negative Feedback in Politics," In *Policy Dynamics*, edited by Frank R. Baumgartner and Bryan D. Jones, 3–28. Chicago: University of Chicago Press.

Baumgartner, Frank R., and Beth L. Leech. 1998. *Basic Interests: The Importance of Groups in Politics and in Political Science*. Princeton, NJ: Princeton University Press.

Behnken, Brian D. 2011. *Fighting Their Own Battles: Mexican Americans, African Americans, and the Struggle for Civil Rights in Texas*. Chapel Hill: University of North Carolina Press.

Berry, Jeffrey M. 1999. *The New Liberalism: The Rising Power of Citizen Groups.* Washington, DC: Brookings Institution Press.

Berry, Jeffrey M., with David Arons. 2003. *A Voice for Nonprofits.* Washington, DC: Brookings Institution Press.

Bositis, David A. 1994. *The Congressional Black Caucus in the 103rd Congress.* Washington, DC: Joint Center for Political and Economic Studies.

Brown, Michael K. 1999. *Race, Money, and the American Welfare State.* Ithaca, NY: Cornell University Press.

Brown, Nadia E. 2014. *Sisters in the Statehouse: Black Women and Legislative Decision Making.* New York: Oxford University Press.

Brown, Nadia E., Michael D. Minta, and Valeria Sinclair-Chapman. 2016. "Personal Narratives and Representation Strategies: Using C-SPAN Oral Histories to Examine Key Concepts in Minority Representation." In *Exploring the C-SPAN Archives: Advancing the Research Agenda,* edited by Robert X. Browning, 139–164. West Lafayette, IN: Purdue University Press.

Cameron, Charles, David Epstein, and Sharyn O'Halloran. 1996. "Do Majority-Minority Districts Maximize Substance Black Representation in Congress?" *American Political Science Review* 90: 794–812.

Canon, David T. 1999. *Race, Redistricting, and Representation: The Unintended Consequences of Black Majority Districts.* Chicago: University of Chicago Press.

Carmines, Edward G., and James A. Stimson. 1989. *Issue Evolution: Race and the Transformation of American Politics.* Princeton, NJ: Princeton University Press.

Casellas, Jason P. 2010. *Latino Representation in State Houses and Congress.* New York: Cambridge University Press.

Chauhan, Preeti, Magdalena Cerdá, Steven F. Messner, Melissa Tracy, Kenneth Tardiff, and Sandro Galea. 2011. "Race/Ethnic-Specific Homicide Rates in New York City: Evaluating the Impact of Broken Windows Policing and Crack Cocaine Markets." *Homicide Studies* 15: 268–90.

Clark, Christopher J. 2019. *Gaining Voice: The Causes and Consequences of Black Representation in the American States.* New York: Oxford University Press.

Clay, William L. 1993. *Just Permanent Interests: Black Americans in Congress 1870–1992.* New York: Amistad Press.

Cohen, Cathy J. 1999. *The Boundaries of Blackness: AIDS and the Breakdown of Black Politics.* Chicago: University of Chicago Press.

Crayton, Kareem U. 2002. "What's New about the New South?" PhD diss., Stanford University.

C-SPAN (Producer). 2009. *Louis Stokes Oral History Interview,* October 25. http://www.c-span.org/video/?289321-1/louis-stokes-oral-history-interview.

———. 2012. *Norman Mineta Oral History Interview,* September 1. https://www.c-span.org/video/?307671-1/norman-mineta-oral-history-interview.

Davidson, Chandler, and Bernard Grofman, editors. 1994. *Quiet Revolution in the South: The Impact of the Voting Rights Act, 1965–1990.* Princeton, NJ: Princeton University Press.

Dawson, Michael C. 2001. *Black Visions: The Roots of Contemporary African-American Political Ideologies.* Chicago: University of Chicago Press.

DeWitt, Larry. 2010. "The Decision to Exclude Agricultural and Domestic Workers from the 1935 Social Security Act." *Social Security Administration, Research, Statistics and Policy Analysis* 70 (4): https://www.ssa.gov/policy/docs/ssb/v70n4/v70n4p49.html.

Dovi, Suzanne. 2002. "Preferable Descriptive Representatives: Will Just Any Woman, Black, or Latino Do?" *American Political Science Review* 96: 729–43.

Falcón, Angelo. 2014. *Immigration Reform and the Latino Civil Rights Movement: Are They Now in Conflict?* New York: National Institute for Latino Policy.

Fenno, Richard. 1978. *Home Style: House Members in Their Districts.* Boston: Little, Brown, and Co.

Fiorina, Morris P. 1974. *Representatives, Roll Calls, and Constituencies.* Lexington, MA: Lexington Books.

Foner, Eric. 1988. *Reconstruction: America's Unfinished Revolution, 1863–1877.* New York: Harper and Row.

Fortner, Michael J. 2015. *Black Silent Majority: The Rockefeller Drug Laws and the Politics of Punishment.* Cambridge, MA: Harvard University Press.

Francis, Megan Ming. 2014. *Civil Rights and the Making of the Modern American State.* New York: Cambridge University Press.

Frymer, Paul. 1999. *Uneasy Alliances: Race and Party Competition in America.* Princeton, NJ: Princeton University Press.

Gamble, Katrina L. 2007. "Black Political Representation: An Examination of Legislative Activity within U.S. House Committees." *Legislative Studies Quarterly* 32: 421–47.

Garcia Bedolla, Lisa. 2009. *Latino Politics.* Cambridge, UK: Polity Press.

Gibson, Campbell, and Kay Jung. 2002. *Historical Census Statistics on Population Totals by Race, 1790 to 1990, and by Hispanic Origin, 1970 to 1990, for the United States, Regions, Divisions, and States.* Washington, DC: U.S. Census Bureau.

Gillion, Daniel Q. 2013. *The Political Power of Protest: Minority Activism and Shifts in Public Policy.* New York: Cambridge University Press.

Grenzke, Janet. 1989. "Shopping in the Congressional Supermarket." *American Political Science Review* 33: 1–24.

Grofman, Bernard, ed. 1998. *Race and Redistricting in the 1990s.* New York: Agathon Press.

Grofman, Bernard, Lisa Handley, and Richard G. Niemi. 1992. *Minority Representation and the Quest for Voting Equality.* New York: Cambridge University Press.

Grose, Christian. 2011. *Congress in Black and White: Race and Representation in Washington and at Home.* New York: Cambridge University Press.

Guinier, Lani. 1994. *The Tyranny of the Majority: Fundamental Fairness in Representative Democracy.* New York: Free Press.

Hancock, Ange-Marie. 2004. *The Politics of Disgust: The Public Identity of the Welfare Queen.* New York: New York University Press.

Haines, Herbert H. 1984. "Black Radicalization and the Funding of Civil Rights: 1957–1970." *Social Problems* 32: 31–43.

Hall, Richard L. 1996. *Participation in Congress.* New Haven, CT: Yale University Press.

Hall, Richard L., and Alan V. Deardorff. 2006. "Lobbying as a Legislative Subsidy." *American Political Science Review* 100: 69–84.

Hall, Richard L., and Frank W. Wayman. 1990. "Buying Time: Moneyed Interests and the Mobilization of Bias in Congressional Committees." *American Political Science Review* 84: 797–820.

Hamilton, Charles V. 1991. *Adam Clayton Powell, Jr.: The Political Biography of an American Dilemma.* New York: Cooper Square Press.

Hansen, John Mark. 1991. *Gaining Access: Congress and the Farm Lobby, 1919–1981.* Chicago: University of Chicago Press.

Hardy-Fanta, Carol, Pei-te Lien, Dianne Pinderhughes, and Christine Maria Sierra. 2016.

Contested Transformation: Race, Gender, and Political Leadership in 21st Century America. New York: Cambridge University Press.

Henry, Charles. 1977. "Legitimizing Race in Congressional Politics." *American Politics Quarterly* 5: 149–76.

Hero, Rodney E. 1992. *Latinos and the U.S. Political System: Two-Tiered Pluralism.* Philadelphia: Temple University Press.

Hero, Rodney E., and Robert R. Preuhs. 2013. *Black-Latino Relations in U.S. National Politics: Beyond Conflict or Cooperation.* Cambridge: Cambridge University Press.

Hero, Rodney E., and Caroline J. Tolbert. 1995. "Latinos and Substantive Representation in the U.S. House of Representatives: Direct, Indirect, or Nonexistent?" *American Journal of Political Science* 39: 640–52.

Hojnacki, Marie, and David Kimball. 1998. "Organized Interests and the Decision of Whom to Lobby in Congress." *American Political Science Review* 92: 775–90.

Hojnacki, Marie, and David Kimball. 2001. "PAC Contributions and Lobbying Contacts in Congressional Committees." *Political Research Quarterly* 54: 161–80.

Humes, Karen R., Nicholas Jones, and Roberto Ramirez. 2011. *Overview of Race and Hispanic Origin. 2010 Census Briefs.* Washington, DC: U.S. Census Bureau.

James, Scott C., and Brian L. Lawson. 1999. "The Political Economy of Voting Rights Enforcement in America's Gilded Age: Electoral College Competition, Partisan Commitment, and the Federal Election Law." *American Political Science Review* 93: 115–31.

Jones, Bryan D., and Frank R. Baumgartner. 2005. *The Politics of Attention: How Government Prioritizes Problems.* Chicago: University of Chicago Press.

Juenke, Eric Gonzalez, and Robert R. Preuhs. 2012. "Irreplaceable Legislators: Rethinking Minority Representatives in the New Century." *American Journal of Political Science* 56 (3): 705–15.

Kanthak, Kristin, and George A. Krause. 2012. *The Diversity Paradox: Political Parties, Legislatures, and the Organizational Foundations of Representation in America.* New York: Oxford University Press.

Kaplowitz, Craig A. 2005. *LULAC, Mexican Americans and National Policy.* College Station: Texas A&M University Press.

Kim, Claire Jean. 2000. *Bitter Fruit: The Politics of Black-Korean Conflict in New York City.* New Haven, CT: Yale University Press.

Kingdon, John W. 1989. *Congressmen's Voting Decisions.* 3rd ed. Ann Arbor: University of Michigan Press.

King-Meadows, Tyson D. 2011. *When the Letter Betrays the Spirit: Voting Rights Enforcement and African American Participation for Lyndon Johnson to Barack Obama.* Lanham, MD: Lexington Books.

Kousser, J. Morgan. 1999. *Colorblind Injustice: Minority Voting Rights and the Undoing of the Second Reconstruction.* Chapel Hill: University of North Carolina Press.

Krehbiel, Keith. 1991. *Information and Legislative Organization. Michigan Studies in Political Analysis.* Ann Arbor: University of Michigan Press.

Krutz, Glen S. 2005. "Issues and Institutions: 'Winnowing' in the U.S. Congress." *American Journal of Political Science* 49: 313–26.

Lee, Frances. 2016. *Insecure Majorities: Congress and the Perpetual Campaign.* Chicago: University of Chicago Press.

Lublin, David. 1997. *The Paradox of Representation: Racial Gerrymandering and Minority Interests in Congress.* Princeton, NJ: Princeton University Press.

Mansbridge, Jane. 1999. "Should Blacks Represent Blacks and Women Represent Women? A Contingent 'Yes.'" *Journal of Politics* 61: 628–57.

Marquez, Benjamin. 1993. *LULAC: The Evolution of a Mexican American Political Organization*. Austin: University of Texas Press.

———. 2003. "Mexican-American Political Organizations and Philanthropy: Bankrolling a Social Movement." *Social Service Review* 77: 329–46.

Martinez, Deirdre. 2009. *Who Speaks for Hispanics? Hispanic Interest Groups in Washington*. Albany: State University of New York Press.

McAdam, Doug. 1982. *Political Process and the Development of Black Insurgency*. Chicago: University of Chicago Press.

McCarty, Nolan, Keith T. Poole, and Howard Rosenthal. 2006. *Polarized America: The Dance of Ideology and Unequal Riches*. Cambridge, MA: MIT Press.

Miller, Warren E., and Donald E. Stokes. 1963. "Constituency Influence in Congress." *American Political Science Review* 57: 45–56.

Minkoff, Debra C. 1999. "Bending with the Wind: Strategic Change and Adaptation by Women's and Racial Minority Organizations." *American Journal of Sociology* 104: 1666–1703.

Minta, Michael D. 2009. "Legislative Oversight and the Substantive Representation of Black and Latino Interests in Congress." *Legislative Studies Quarterly* 34: 193–218.

———. 2011. *Oversight: Representing Black and Latino Interests in Congress*. Princeton, NJ: Princeton University Press.

Minta, Michael D., and Nadia E. Brown. 2014. "Intersecting Interests: Gender, Race, and Congressional Attention to Women's Issues." *Du Bois Review: Social Science Research on Race* 11: 253–72.

Minta, Michael D., and Valeria Sinclair-Chapman. 2013. "Diversity in Congress and Institutional Responsiveness, 1951–2004." *Political Research Quarterly* 66: 127–39.

Mora, G. Cristina. 2014. *Making Hispanics: How Activists, Bureaucrats, and Media Constructed a New American*. Chicago: University of Chicago Press.

Morris, Aldon D. 1984. *The Origins of the Civil Rights Movement: Black Communities Organizing for Change*. New York: Free Press.

Murakawa, Naomi. 2014. *The First Civil Right: How Liberal Built Prison America*. New York: Oxford University Press.

Overby, L. Marvin, and Kenneth M. Cosgrove. 1996. "Unintended Consequences? Racial Redistricting and the Representation of Minority Interests." *Journal of Politics* 58: 540–50.

Paden, Catherine M. 2011. *Civil Rights Advocacy on Behalf of the Poor*. Philadelphia: University Pennsylvania Press.

Pinderhughes, Dianne M. 1995. "Black Interest Groups and the 1982 Extension of the Voting Rights Act." In *Blacks and the American Political System*, edited by H. L. Perry, 203–24. Gainesville: University Press of Florida.

Piven, Frances Fox, and Richard A. Cloward. 1977. *Poor People's Movements: Why They Succeed and How They Fail*. New York: Pantheon Books.

Rivers, Christina R. 2012. *The Congressional Black Caucus, Minority Voting Rights, and the U.S. Supreme Court*. Ann Arbor: University of Michigan Press.

Rouse, Stella M. 2013. *Latinos in the Legislative Process: Interests and Influence*. New York: Cambridge University Press.

Schattschneider, E. E. 1960. *The Semisovereign People; A Realist's View of Democracy in America*. New York: Holt, Rinehart and Winston.

Schickler, Eric. 2016. *Racial Realignment: The Transformation of American Liberalism, 1932–1965*. Princeton, NJ: Princeton University Press.

Schiller, Wendy. 2000. *Partners and Rivals: Representation in U.S. Senate Delegations*. Princeton, NJ: Princeton University Press.

Schlozman, Kay Lehman. 1984. "What Accent the Heavenly Chorus? Political Equality and the American Pressure System." *Journal of Politics* 46: 1006–32.

Schlozman, Kay Lehman, and John T. Tierney. 1986. *Organized Interests and American Democracy*. New York: Harper and Row.

Schlozman, Kay Lehman, Sidney Verba, and Henry E. Brady. 2012. *The Unheavenly Chorus: Unequal Political Voice and the Broken Promise of American Democracy*. Princeton, NJ: Princeton University Press.

Shepsle, Kenneth A. 1978. *The Giant Jigsaw Puzzle: Democratic Committee Assignments in the Modern House*. Chicago: University of Chicago Press.

Shotts, Kenneth W. 2003. "Does Racial Redistricting Cause Conservative Policy Outcomes? Policy Preferences of Southern Representatives in the 1980s and 1990s." *Journal of Politics* 65: 216–26.

Singh, Robert. 1998. *The Congressional Black Caucus: Racial Politics in the U.S. Congress*. Thousand Oaks, CA: Sage Publications.

Smith, Mark A. 2000. *American Business and Political Power: Public Opinion, Elections, and Democracy*. Chicago: University of Chicago Press.

Smith, Robert. 1996. *We Have No Leaders: African-Americans in the Post–Civil Rights Era*. Albany: State University of New York Press.

Strach, Patricia. 2016. *Hiding Politics in Plain Sight: Cause Marketing, Corporate Influence, and Breast Cancer Marketing*. New York: Oxford University Press.

Strolovitch, Dara Z. 2007. *Affirmative Advocacy: Race, Class, and Gender in Interest Group Politics*. Chicago: University of Chicago Press.

Sullivan, Patricia. 2009. *Lift Every Voice: The NAACP and the Making of the Civil Rights Movement*. New York: New Press.

Sulkin, Tracy. 2005. *Issue Politics in Congress*. New York: Cambridge University Press.

Swain, Carol M. 1993. *Black Faces, Black Interests: The Representation of African Americans in Congress*. Cambridge, MA: Harvard University Press.

Tate, Katherine. 2003. *Black Faces in the Mirror: African Americans and Their Representatives in the U.S. Congress*. Princeton, NJ: Princeton University Press.

———. 2010. *What's Going On?: Political Incorporation and the Transformation of Black Public Opinion*. Washington, DC: Georgetown University Press.

———. 2014. *Concordance: Black Lawmaking in the U.S. Congress from Carter to Obama*. Ann Arbor: University of Michigan Press.

Thernstrom, Abigail. 1987. *Whose Votes Count? Affirmative Action and Minority Voting Rights*. Cambridge, MA: Harvard University Press.

Tichenor, Daniel J. 2002. *Dividing Lines: The Politics of Immigration Control in America*. Princeton, NJ: Princeton University Press.

Tillery, Alvin B. 2011. *Between Homeland and Motherland: Africa, U.S. Foreign Policy, and Black Leadership in America*. Ithaca, NY: Cornell University Press.

Truman, David B. 1971. *The Governmental Process: Political Interests and Public Opinion*. 2nd ed. New York: Knopf.

Ture, Kwame, and Charles V. Hamilton. 1967. *Black Power: The Politics of Liberation in America*. New York: Random House.

Tyson, Vanessa C. 2016. *Twists of Fate: Multiracial Coalitions and Minority Representation in the U.S. House of Representatives*. New York: Oxford University Press.

U.S. Congress, House Committee on Appropriations. 1997. *Departments of Labor, Health and Human Services, Education and Related Agencies Appropriations of 1998: Hearing before a Subcommittee on Appropriations.* 105th Cong., 1st sess., April 24. Statement of Rep. Rubén Hinojosa.

U.S. Congress, House Committee on Financial Services. 2007. *Legislative Proposals Reforming Mortgage Practices: Hearing before the Committee on Financial Services.* 110th Cong., 1st sess., October 24.

U.S. Congress, Committee on Government Reform and Oversight. 1997. *Federal Measures of Race and Ethnicity and the Implications for the 2000 Census: Hearings before the Subcommittee on Government Management, Information, and Technology.* 105th Cong., 1st sess., April 23, May 22, and July 25.

U.S. Congress, Committee on the Judiciary. 1995. *Cocaine and Federal Sentencing Policy. Hearing before the Subcommittee on Crime.* 104th Cong,. 1st sess., June 29 (statement of Wade Henderson, NAACP's main lobbyist).

U.S. Congress, Committee on the Judiciary. 2007. *Comprehensive Immigration Reform: Perspectives from Faith-Based and Immigrant Communities: Hearing before the Subcommittee on Immigration, Citizenship, Refugees, Border Security, and International Law.* 110th Cong., 1st sess., May 22.

U.S. Congress, Committee on Ways and Means. 1935. *Economic Security Act: Hearing before the Committee on Ways and Means.* 74th Cong., 1st sess., January 21–26, 28–31, and February 1–2, 4–8, and 12.

———. 2008. *Addressing Disparities in Health and Healthcare: Issues of Reform: Hearing before the Subcommittee on Health.* 110th Cong., 2nd sess., June 10.

U.S. Congress, Select Committee on Narcotics Abuse and Control and Select Committee on Children, Youth, and Families. 1986. *The Crack Cocaine Crisis: Joint Hearing before the Select Committee on Narcotics Abuse and Control and Select Committee on Children, Youth, and Families.* 99th Cong., 2nd sess., July 15.

Valelly, Richard M. 2004. *The Two Reconstructions: The Struggle for Black Enfranchisement.* Chicago: University of Chicago Press.

Volden, Craig, and Alan E. Wiseman. 2014. *Legislative Effectiveness in the United States Congress: The Lawmakers.* New York: Cambridge University Press.

Walker, Jack L. 1983. "The Origins and Maintenance of Interest Groups in America." *American Political Science Review* 77: 390–406.

Walker, Jack L., Jr. 1991. *Mobilizing Interest Groups in America: Patrons, Professions, and Social Movements.* Ann Arbor: University of Michigan Press.

Wallace, Sophia J. 2014. "Representing Latinos: Examining Descriptive and Substantive Representation in Congress." *Political Research Quarterly* 67: 917–29.

Walton, Hanes, Jr. 1988. *When the Marching Stopped: The Politics of Civil Rights Regulatory Agencies.* Albany: State University of New York.

Walton, Hanes, Jr., and Robert C. Smith. 2000. *American Politics and the African American Quest for Universal Freedom.* New York: Pearson Longman.

Watson, Denton L. 1990. *Lion in the Lobby: Clarence Mitchell, Jr.'s Struggle for the Passage of Civil Rights Laws.* Lanham, MD: University Press Association.

Weingast, Barry R., and William J. Marshall. 1988. "The Industrial Organization of Congress; or, Why Legislatures, Like Firms, Are Not Organized as Markets." *Journal of Political Economy* 96: 132–63.

Weiss, Nancy J. 1974. *The National Urban League, 1910–1940.* New York: Oxford University Press.

Whitby, Kenny J. 1997. *The Color of Representation: Congressional Behavior and Black Interests*. Ann Arbor: University of Michigan Press.

Wilson, Walter Clark. 2017. *From Inclusion to Influence: Latino Representation in Congress and Latino Political Incorporation in America*. Ann Arbor: University of Michigan Press.

Wong, Carolyn. 2006. *Lobbying for Inclusion: Rights Politics and the Making of Immigration Policy*. Stanford, CA: Stanford University Press.

Zelizer, Julian E. 2004. *On Capitol Hill: The Struggle to Reform Congress and Its Consequences, 1948–2000*. New York: Cambridge University Press.

INDEX

Page numbers in *italics* refer to figures and tables.